THEA RØNNING

YOUNG WOMAN ON A MISSION

Gracia Grindal

Lutheran University Press
Minneapolis, Minnesota

THEA RØNNING
Young Woman on a Mission
By Gracia Grindal

Copyright 2012 Gracia Grindal. All rights reserved. Published by Lutheran University Press, an imprint of 1517 Media. Except for brief quotations in critical articles or reviews, no part of this book may be reproduced in any manner without prior written permission from the publisher.

Library of Congress Cataloging-in-Publication Data

Grindal, Gracia.
  Thea Rønning : young woman on a mission / Gracia Grindal.
      pages cm
  Includes bibliographical references (p.   ) and index.
  ISBN 978-1-932688-79-5 (alk. paper) -- ISBN 1-932688-79-X (alk. paper) -- eISBN 978-1-942304-94-4
  1. Rønning, Thea, 1865-1898. 2. Missionaries--China--Biography. 3. Missionaries--Norway--Biography. 4. Missions--China. 5. Lutheran Church--Missions. I. Title.
  BV3427.R563G75 2012
  266'.41092--dc23
  [B]
                                        2012043018

Dedicated to my aunts, my father's sisters, known to their father, Svein Kivle, as the Kivle maidens, *Kivlemøyane*—Mabel, Marion, Matilda, Myrtle Kivle and their husbands, Joseph Werdal, Morris Werdal, Tommy Nortvedt, Morris Larson, and our Norwegian cousin Per Kivle and his wife, Torveig, whose service to mission work in China and Japan introduced me to the life and adventure of bringing Christ to the nations, especially China.

CONTENTS

Preface 6
Introduction 8
Torbjørg (Thea) Nilsdatter Rønning (1865-1898) 11
China's Millions 13
Thea's Call 26
Newcomers in the New Land 30
Ladies Aids and Missions 37
The O. S. Nestegaard Brothers 49
Thea's Norwegian Roots... 65
The Journey to China 66
Arrival in China 78
Sailing Up the Yangzi to Hankow 80
Hankow 82
Settling In 92
Life Together.. 99
New Friends Arrive 107
Establishing the Fancheng Station 113
The China Thea Experienced... 127
Getting Organized at Home and in China 128
The Women's Work Takes Hold 142
Heat, Illness, and Danger 150
Thea Meets Landahl 154
Engagement, Near Death, Marriage, and Honeymoon 166
Thea Comes into Her Own 175
Taipingdian 182
Afterword 193
Appendix 196
Endnotes 199
Index 209

PREFACE

This book began nearly thirty years ago when Bonnie Jensen of the American Lutheran Church Women asked me to prepare a slide/tape presentation on the life of a woman missionary. I had just come to Luther Seminary to study and teach.

One of my projects had been to examine the life and times of Thea (Torbjørg) Rønning, a young woman from Norway who came to America and then a few years later left with her brother, Halvor, to work on the mission field in China for the Hauge Synod. I had always admired the Rønning family and was surprised to find so many materials in the little-known journals of the Hauge Synod, mostly letters from the missionaries that were as intimate and revealing as their private letters home. From them I could construct a life that was brief and little-remembered except by family.

Over the years I have continued to research Thea's life and work. Some time ago an old friend, Øyvind Gulliksen—professor emeritus of American studies at Telemark University College, Bø Telemark, Norway, where the Rønnings were born and raised—spoke with me about our shared interest in the Rønnings. He said he thought he could find private letters from her on the farm where she grew up. Later he wrote me to say he had indeed found letters and would be happy to send them, or at least have them ready any time I would come to visit the farm. Last year while on sabbatical, I visited the farm to see the letters firsthand. With that it was easy to begin the book, parts of which had been written before.

At first it had been intended to be a only a chapter in a larger book on women in the Norwegian-American Lutheran churches, but the amount of material available seemed to indicate that a larger work was more appropriate, especially since most of the material is in Norwegian and most Americans, even her family in America, can no longer read the language. It is my hope that the book will reintroduce people to the life of women missionaries, the growth of the Ladies Aids among Norwegian-American Lutherans, and some of the heroes and heroines whose dedication unto their own death planted seeds in China that are still growing and being harvested by the great-great-grandchildren of their first converts in China. As I read their frequent comments on the untimely death of a colleague, that the blood of the martyrs is the seed of the church, I realized I was observing the planting of many seeds which in the words of Psalm 126 were "sown in tears, but now are being harvested with rejoicing."

There are many people to thank: first the American Lutheran Church Women, then the late Della Olson of the archives at Luther Seminary who found arcane histories of the circles and Ladies Aids for me. Professor Gulliksen's interests were also helpful as he directed me to the sources. Paul Rorem, editor of *The Lutheran Quarterly* has continued to encourage me to tell this story. As the book took shape, Charlotte Martinson Gronseth and Paul Martinson, grandchild and child of missionaries to China read and commented on the manuscript. Paul Ofstedal, the former head of China Venture Services, has encouraged the work as well by asking me to speak on Thea's life and work at their meetings. Both he and his wife, Dorthea, have read the manuscript and offered helpful comments. Whatever errors there are in the book, however, are completely mine.

Without the support of Luther Seminary—the administration and faculty, and the board of directors who granted me a sabbatical to research and write on this topic among others—this project could never have been completed. Victoria Smith, the faculty secretary, and Kari Bostrom in the Luther Seminary archives have been faithful helpers as I have worked to garner these resources, hidden far back in the 1890s. I am grateful to them all for their support. Without their encouragement and the assurance that it would be published, I would not have dared to spend the time and energy to finish it.

INTRODUCTION

To discover late in my life that my first literary hero, Nils N. Rønning (1869-1962), had a sister, Thea, who became a missionary to China, was, on a somewhat smaller scale, rather like Virginia Woolf musing on what it would have been like to discover that Shakespeare had a sister. As a young girl and a voracious reader, I had been thrilled to read Rønning's account of his growing up in Bø in Telemark, Norway, not far from my grandfather Svein Torson Kivle's birthplace near Seljord in Kivledalen, a storied place in Norwegian legend and history. In his book, *A Boy from Telemark*, Rønning had even told the story of the Kivle maidens (*Kivlemøyane*) who had been turned to stone by the pastor in the parish when he saw them participating in pagan ceremonies outside the stone church in the mountains near the farm.

Hungry for stories about my people, I read his books over and over again, especially *A Boy from Telemark* and *Fifty Years in America* for their accounts of people I had heard about from my parents: the Sverdrups, Oftedals, Kildahls, etc. My mother told of having met Rønning while riding on a train from Minneapolis to her home near Morris, Minnesota, in the late 1930s and talking with him about Norwegians, especially those from Telemark, her father's ancestral county in Norway. He described the Telemark soul as being like a valley of sorrow through which a river of joy flowed. The poverty and beauty of the home place with the mountains behind and the river below becomes vivid when you stand on the Rønning farm where the siblings grew up. The image had moved me when I was a young reader and teenager, wondering about my own heritage.

In the summer of 1962, I began working as a nurses' aide for $0.95 an hour at Field Hall, a building in the complex known as Ebenezer Old People's Home in Minneapolis, founded and run by Norwegian Lutherans. My first day I heard the nurses grieving the death of one of their favorite patients. When I asked who it was, they told me he was N. N. Rønning. Although I had never met him, I lamented the missed opportunity and took it as something of a passing on to me of his literary mantle. I would have loved to have spoken with him about his writing and his place in the literary and church world in which I had grown up. He knew it all very well, and as Christian writer, publisher, and educator had helped shape it.

Twenty years later, while studying and teaching at Luther Seminary, I decided to write a paper on women missionaries, especially those who had gone to China. In doing so I could learn both something about the worldwide mission movement of the Christian church in the nineteenth century and about women who served as missionaries, especially those with a passion to save souls in China. China meant romance and intrigue to me. I had read a biography of Hudson Taylor and never had forgotten it. The romance of China had attracted me, as it did for many others at the time. Ever since I was small, I had heard about it from my uncle, Morris Werdal, who had been born in China to a Norwegian-American father and mother who were missionaries there. My father would tell of Mrs. Werdal, the mother-in-law of his two sisters, who had lost her foot in a farm accident when she ran out to her father mowing his fields and did not see the mower's blade in the grass. Dad said she was the greatest preacher he had ever heard, and the story of her refusing to be kept from the mission field despite a wooden leg filled him with wonder.

During a week-long Epiphany mission festival in Rugby one year in the 1950s while the temperature plummeted to a negative forty degrees, Uncle Morris and Lenorah Erickson, now exiled from China by the Bamboo Curtain, talked of their time in China. Then China seemed as far away as the moon. Miss Erickson taught me how to write some Chinese characters, and Uncle Morris told me how Chiang Kai Shek, a friend of Christian missionaries, suggested his father be buried in the little Protestant graveyard near his residence. It was pure romance and adventure. My research began when I read several books on the China mission and the Norwegian-Americans who served there, then read the religious periodicals of the day, especially *Kinamissionæren* (*The China Missionary*) put out by the China Mission society in America. I did know from N. N. Rønning's writings that he had a brother, Halvor Nilsen

(1869-1962), who had gone to China. We knew of his son, Chester (1894-1984), who became head of the Canadian legation to China from 1941 to 1951, and other Rønnings, such as Halvor who lives in Jerusalem and was a guide to many of the tours that came from Luther Seminary to the Holy Land. It was a distinguished family.

To discover, however, that they had a sister, Thea (1865-1898), who had gone with her brother Halvor to China in 1891, surprised me and sent me in pursuit of her life and story. Brief and tragic as it was, it could help me tell the story of the early missionaries to China from the Norwegian-American churches and at the same time help me understand how it was that young women who did not appear to have a direct route into the parsonage, and who did not see herself as a member of the clergy class, could yet, by the end of the nineteenth century, enter into a kind of professional ministry that was very like that of a pastor. Her story showed not just how the elite women in the parsonage or professors' families lived out their Christian callings as the modern era began to dawn, but also how the women from the non-elite classes of their day began to serve the church in ways that could be considered almost as public as that of their pastor brothers.

TORBJØRG (THEA) NILSDATTER RØNNING (1865-1898)

Torbjørg (Thea) Nilsdatter Rønning (1865-1898) was born on the Buskerønning farm, to parents who owned the farm, but struggled to eke out an existence on it. It was just outside the town of Bø in Telemark, near the southern shores of Seljord Lake (Seljordvatn), an inland fjord between the mountains in the central county of Norway. To look up at the mountain rising behind the farm and hear the fresh rush of waters sweeping down the mountains into the river below the farm is to know what the young girl saw and heard as she was growing up in Norway's scenic beauty and grinding poverty. To see the old medieval church where she was baptized, the newer nineteenth-century church where she was confirmed, and remember what she and her brothers did to further the gospel in America and then China, is to marvel at how God fulfills God's purposes with the simplest of means and people.

Thea Rønning

Torbjørg (Thea) Nilsdatter Rønning and her two brothers, Nils Nilson and Halvor Nilson, immigrated to America in the 1880s. All three distinguished themselves in God's service. Nils and Halvor were well known in the world in which I grew up. But not their sister.

To tell the story of Thea and her burning desire to minister to Chinese women, whose lives by most accounts were filled with oppression and cruelty, it is also necessary to tell the story of how she learned of the needs in China, the establishment of the mission society that sent her, and the Ladies Aids from whom she garnered interest and support. The women in the Midwestern Norwegian-American churches who supported her and the entire mission with their gatherings, dinners, bazaars, surprise parties, and fishponds, at a time when a few nickels could make the difference between life and death in China, played no small part in her life and work. Their work to bring the gospel to women in China through women like Thea needs to be told. It shows that the lady missionary's vocation was a worthy profession, one she and her women colleagues, married or unmarried, filled with passion and unrelenting zeal to bring the gospel of Jesus Christ and salvation to the Chinese women. Their work is still bearing fruit today as millions of Chinese people for whom they had come to care so deeply are joyfully accepting the good news of Jesus Christ.

CHINA'S MILLIONS

When James Hudson Taylor (1832-1905) was in his mother's womb, his parents, James and Amalia Taylor, both faithful English Methodists infatuated with the Far East, dedicated their firstborn son to the Lord. They thought much about China, and their enthusiasm for it transferred to their son who, upon reading a book on China, conceived a passion for that far-away land. His parent's prayers were answered. After his conversion as a teenager, Taylor began to prepare for life as a missionary to China. In addition to a deeper searching of the Bible during this time, he studied both medicine and Mandarin Chinese. He sailed for China as a young man of twenty-two, arriving on March 1, 1854. He made the decision to "go native." He wore Chinese clothes and grew the traditional pigtail of the Chinese man in order to show his love for the Chinese.

Young Hudson Taylor

When Taylor arrived, China was entering a period of enormous chaos and upheaval. Its social structures of over 2,000 years were being called into question by those who wanted to modernize or "westernize" their country, or at the very least reform it so that the mandate of heaven would return, something the Qing dynasty had lost. Still in the grips of the old Confucian order, China was tottering partly because of the corruption of the Confucian bureaucracy and the byzantine system it had developed over thousands of years. Order was maintained, if at all, by violent robber chiefs and local mandarins. Flood and famine ravaged the land, as they had for centuries, so that millions of people starved to death or died from rampant epidemics caused by indescribably unsanitary conditions. If people did not die young of natural disasters or disease, many often sought to escape these conditions with opium following China's defeat in the Opium War in 1842.

The war had begun when China tried to stop British merchants from selling opium in the country which had been imported from India, but the war ended badly for the Chinese. Their loss produced The Treaty of Nanjing (1842) which granted the British the right to sell the opium in China, trading it for silk and other products from the East, and at the same time causing many Chinese to become addicted to a substance which would help keep China dissolute and unable to defend itself. The same treaty also granted the British the Hong Kong colony, the right to send missionaries to China, and the guarantee of extra-territorial rights for their citizens: that is, British citizens could live in some places in China and were not subject to Chinese law. The treaty was an insult to the dignity of the Chinese who rarely let the missionaries forget that they came to China at the same time as opium.

In 1854, the year of Taylor's arrival, China was in a state of total war as a result of the Taiping Rebellion, a vicious civil war. The leader, Hong Xiuquan (1814-1864), had met Liang Fa (1789-1855), a native evangelist, who was distributing Christian tracts by the London Bible Society. It was the practice of the Bible Society to give tracts and Bibles to the ambitious young men taking the difficult examinations on their way to becoming mandarins. They hoped the Chinese would become Christians and as leaders help to evangelize China. Hong Xiuquan laid these materials aside until 1843, when upon the questioning of a cousin, he took them up again and found them to be the truth. He saw their message as a way to cleanse China of its corruption. He and his cousin baptized themselves, threw out their Confucian idols, and took up the sword after he decided he was the younger brother of Jesus Christ. The war he and his followers prosecuted from 1851-1864 was the bloodiest war of any in the world during the nineteenth century. In some ways it was a rebellion of the Han people against the Manchu dynasty. The Han considered themselves more Chinese than the Manchu of the Qing Dynasty who were then in power. Hong and his soldiers took much of China, especially south of the Yangzi River, and built their headquarters in Nanjing. The European powers, primarily Great Britain and America, became enmeshed in the struggle especially after the emperor allowed British soldiers in captivity to be brutally treated in prison, in ways that Lord Elgin, the commander of the English forces, found to be unworthy of gentlemen. (He was the son of the Lord Elgin who confiscated the marble frieze on the Parthenon.) In order to teach the emperor and his minions a lesson, Lord Elgin ordered his soldiers to burn down the historic Summer Palace in October 1860. The loss to the historical treasury of China was incalculable, but he is said to have done it to save lives. It took two days for the huge complex of buildings, palaces, libraries, and art to burn. It temporarily shocked the residents in the Forbidden City.

The Confucian way of life held up honesty, reverenced the past, and taught respect for parents and the emperor. This system served to maintain the dynasty in power for generations. As long as China remained in its Middle Kingdom mentality with no need for trade or contact with the barbarians outside the kingdom, such as the British, it perpetuated the system. By the middle of the nineteenth century the system still held, and those who tried to undermine it were brutally punished. Clans, or extended families, were held responsible for the wrongdoing of any of their members. Anyone found to be supporting the rebels could be thrown into jail; they could be tortured for any reason ruled appropriate by the mandarins. Beheading was common, as was crucifixion, as well as standing in lime until one's flesh was eaten away to the bone. For minor offenses, the cangue, a kind of portable stocks in which the prisoner would not be able to move his hands to his mouth, making it impossible to eat or drink without help , was used. Treason was by far the most serious of offenses because it involved breaking the fundamental law of Confucianism, reverence for the emperor, the ultimate power. For that crime the traitor could be slowly dismembered.

Getting into a governing office cost enormous expenditures of time and energy. The examinations, held every three years, were too difficult for many, so bribery and corruption became common. This meant that less than competent people could rise to the top in officialdom. Corruption went all the way into the very heart of the Forbidden City where the dynastic rulers lived in almost complete isolation from their people. Other than the emperor, the only men allowed in what was called "the Great Within" were eunuchs. Deprived of progeny by their castration, they lived outside of Chinese ritual life, unable to sacrifice to the ancestors and unable to father children. They developed a culture all their own. The other people in the palace were the concubines from whom the emperor would choose his consort. In many ways he was left without any human companionship of a normal kind. Some have called him, given his isolation, the loneliest man on the planet. Over time the sexual excesses of the palace and the intrigues of the eunuchs debauched the emperor and his family. The Dowager Empress Cixi (1835-1908), who was in power during the last half of the nineteenth century, came from the concubines. Upon her first tryst with the young emperor, she used her beauty and considerable feminine wiles and intellect to gain his affection and finally to use it to gain, as regent, total control of the dynasty by the end of the century.

While the battles in the palace or in the war do not need to be described here, it should be noted that as Hudson Taylor began his work in China, the Taiping Rebellion, which took the lives of some twenty million, was just beginning. The rebels, known as the warriors of the Heavenly Kingdom, had decreed something similar to the Ten Commandments as the basis for their laws: they were sabbatarian, allowed women to fight in the army, unbound the feet of women—most enlightened reformers understood this to be paramount if China was to enter the modern world—and forbad divorce. Even as the imperial army defeated this insurrection with the help of the American, Ward Frederick Townsend (1831-1862) and British General Gordon, Chinese people were coming to believe that the dynasty was collapsing. The Dowager Empress Cixi was still completely in charge of the royal house through her brutal uses of the accoutrements of power, poisoning those who threatened her power, even corrupting her own son, and somehow pilfering the royal seal as the emperor, her own nephew, lay dying of his debauchery.

As the missionaries came in greater and greater numbers, China seemed to be descending further and further into chaos while those dwelling in the imperial palaces ignored the outside world, unable to imagine a situation in which people from other empires would refuse to comply with them. As Westerners increasingly came to China's shores to trade, they brought back tales of both China's fascination and injustice, especially the conditions of women and their bound feet. The needs of China, not only for help but also for the gospel, began to stir many Christians in the West, who organized societies to send and support missionaries to the ancient land.

It should also be noted that the rise of the Heavenly Kingdom and its adoption of an odd variant of Christianity was not the first time Christianity had made an impact on China. Ancient artifacts indicate that Nestorian Christians had been in China from the seventh century during the Tang Dynasty (618-907). Marco Polo (1254-1324) had discovered some of those remnants on his fabled journey there. Pope Innocent in 1245 sent a Franciscan friar to the Mongols to try to persuade them not to continue their sweep into Europe. This resulted in a mission to Mongolia. In 1295, the first Roman Catholic missionaries arrived in China and built a church in Beijing. They founded churches in several Chinese cities and hoped to convert the emperor, but the Chinese considered Christianity a religion for foreigners. The Jesuits later sent emissaries who had considerable impact on China, the first in 1552 when St. Francis Xavier (1506-1552), one of the founders of the Society of Jesus, died on the island of Shangchuan awaiting a chance to enter China. Thirty years later an Italian, Matteo Ricci (1582-1610), brought Western culture to the Chinese court, even beginning an inter-faith dialogue with representatives of Confucianism. Some Chinese, including Confucian scholars, converted to Christianity, even becoming Jesuits. Scholars have estimated that from the death of Xavier until 1800, almost one thousand Jesuits had served in China.[1] A significant number of Franciscans also went to China in the late eighteenth century and suffered martyrdom along with other Christians after the emperor issued a decree against the Catholic faith (which included all other Christians). Not long after the first Opium War there may have been almost 240,000 Roman Catholics in China. Some estimate that by 1901 there were almost one million Chinese Roman Catho-

Matteo Ricci

lics.² Given the suspicion between Protestants and Catholics, Protestants such as Taylor did not give the Catholics much quarter and began their work almost as if there were no Christians in China; in fact they spent some efforts trying to convert Chinese Catholics to their various confessions. On March 1, 1854, when Taylor arrived in Shanghai at one of the five treaty ports that the Chinese opened to Westerners with the Treaty of Nanjing, he joined with other Protestant European missionaries who had already established a beginning mission work, The Chinese Evangelical Society. What he found, however, did not seem to him to be effective in converting Chinese people to the gospel, especially those millions far inland. Taylor was not impressed with the society's approach and began to develop his own strategy for Christianizing China. He left the society in 1857 for Ningbo, one of the oldest cities in China on the shores of the China Sea, also one of the cities taken by the Heavenly Kingdom rebels. There he married an English missionary, Maria Dyer (1837-1870), and began translating the Bible into the Ningbo dialect. By 1861, poor health, probably hepatitis, forced him to return to England for treatment and recovery.

While in England he continued his translating, while studying midwifery. During this time he worked to encourage more people to go to China as missionaries. To that end he wrote a pamphlet, *China: Its Spiritual Need and Claims*, one of the most effective recruiting tools for the mission that has ever been written. At the same time, Taylor began building an organization to bring missionaries to China's inland provinces, calling it the China Inland Mission (CIM) which he established in 1865 after the cessation of the worst hostilities in the rebellion. He recruited young men and women, even single women, to evangelize China's inland where Christianity remained relatively unknown. His missionaries were to go on faith, without salaries, depending on prayer for their financial support. They would show respect for the Chinese by wearing native costumes, and the men would grow the traditional long braid, or queue. When he recovered his health, Taylor returned to China with even more young people preparing to serve in his mission. With his training in midwifery, he was now able to help women during their pregnancies and childbirth while sending his growing number of troops into previously untouched regions of China. By 1876, the China Inland Mission was supporting over fifty missionaries working in all of the provinces of China and Mongolia. Taylor recruited strong people, saying:

> China is not to be won for Christ by quiet, ease-loving men and women. The stamp of men and women we need is such as will put Jesus, China, [and] souls first and foremost in everything and at every time—even life itself must be secondary.[3]

Taylor's mission (CIM) became the most well-known of those in China, and it received support from around the world. His writings were translated into many languages, and his indefatigable travels continued to attract new recruits. Meanwhile others, in response to Taylor's call, began traveling around the world urging young people to go to China to preach the gospel of Jesus Christ. One of the most effective developers of the China Mission in Scandinavia was Fredrik Franson (1852-1910), a Swedish-American

CIM headquarters in London

who had worked with the Moody-Sankey revivals in America. In 1881, he went to Scandinavia to spark greater interest in mission work there. He spent over a year in Norway, visiting cities from north to south, speaking and organizing mission societies. He was especially successful in the southern coast of Norway, a center of religious ferment at the time, in such towns as Skien, Larvig, Drammen, and Kongsberg. Skien, one of the most spiritually lively centers in southern Norway, was a nub of activity for this work. It figures in the story of the Rønnings, especially Halvor who attended school in Skien. In addition, there were many others in their community who also were enthusiastic supporters of mission work, including their schoolteacher and pastor, Johannes Christian Thorvald Crøger (1836-1887).[4]

China's Millions | 19

However, while the concern for missions in Norway was not new, the concern for China was. The KwaZulu area in South Africa was already a well-established field for Norwegians. In 1842, Gustava Kielland (1800-1889), a pastor's wife in Lyngdal, Norway, began a women's missionary society to raise awareness of world missions and actively support them with gifts of money and clothes, after hearing a lecture on missions and regretting the lukewarm attitude of Norwegians toward foreign missions. That year the first Norwegian missionary, Bishop Hans Paludan Smith Schreuder (1817-1882), left Norway for South Africa to serve the KwaZulu people. He became something of a hero for the Norwegians, and when the first Zulu convert, a woman named Umatendhjwaze, was baptized in 1858 after fourteen years of work, church bells rang throughout Norway and the hymnist Magnus Brostrup Landstad (1802-1880) wrote a hymn, "Lift up your hearts, O Christian soul" ("*Oppløft ditt syn, du kristensjel*"), celebrating the event. It was some years later, in the 1880s, that China came to be a burning concern in Norway, along with the new mission field in Madagascar, where both Norwegians and Norwegian-Americans were beginning mission work.

Fredrik Franson

Taylor's mission came to be well known in Scandinavia when emissaries of Taylor had come to Norway. Reginald Radcliffe (1825-1895), a supporter and very close friend of Hudson Taylor, came to Arendal in southern Norway in 1879 to promote Christian causes, especially the mission in China. He had a special concern for the work of women and the necessity for women missionaries who could go to China to work with Chinese women who were most open to the gospel. China's needs, both temporal and spiritual at that time, were well known in Scandinavia as was the call for young people to go. That had resulted in the thrilling story of two young single Norwegian women, Sofie Dorothea Reuter (1860-1891) and

Anna Sofie Jakobson (1860-1913), who in 1884 left Norway to join Taylor and the China Inland Mission in London. Reuter came from Arendal, one of the first congregations in the Lutheran Free Church of Norway, and Jacobson from Kristiansand at the southern tip of Norway. Radcliffe had spoken in the home of Theodor and Elisabeth Rasmussen where Jakobson worked as a maid. This had awakened her to the need in China. The next year when Fredrik Franson traveled through Norway, he had also spoken in the Rasmussen home. Anna had

Reginald Radcliffe

gone to Oslo to receive some training in mission work, and then she and Sofie traveled to London for further training at the local offices of the CIM. Their story as single women with a passion to bring the Gospel of Jesus Christ to China enflamed the spiritually awakened in Norway. When Reuter and Jakobson left Norway in 1884 for London and China in 1885, their letters home were shared, and many Christians in the region knew that even young single women could go to China and serve.

The Norwegian emigrants in America brought these concerns with them. At the time, America was considered by many to be a mission field in itself. Many pastors who did come to America, such as Hans Andreas Stub (1822-1907), at first had felt called to either Africa or America as places to serve. Almost as soon as they had built church buildings in the New World, the Norwegian-Americans wanted to support foreign missions. The pastors suggested they send money to Norway to support the Schreuder mission. Both the Norwegian Synod and the Conference sent pastors back to the annual meeting of the Norwegian Mission Society. The trip became a perk for overworked pastors who used the rest and relaxation afforded by the long journey as a time to visit relatives and friends they had not seen in years, as well as an opportunity to recruit new pastors and professors for work in their American seminaries and congregations. Some of their best recruits became leaders of the young church: Ludvig Marinus Biørn (1835-1908), a leader in the Norwegian Synod, later the Anti-Missourian Brotherhood, and finally the United Church; Georg Sverdrup (1848-1907), Sven Gunnersen (1844-1904), and Sven Oftedal (1844-1911), professors at Augsburg Seminary.[5]

Halvor and Thea, who both went through a kind of spiritual struggle (*anfechtelse*) after their confirmation, had come to assurance of their salvation in their own time, with the help of their pastor Crøger and others, even as they prayed for the salvation of their siblings and parents. By the time peace did come to them, they were thankful that the entire family had also converted. As Halvor put it in his autobiography, while his parents had taught him "about God the Father, Son, and God the Holy Spirit, it had little effect; it was rather like the blind leading the blind."[6] His grade school teacher in religion was a drunk who would come late to school and fall asleep, he said. Halvor's parents, typical members of the state church, were not especially pious, allowing drink and dance in their home. That would change soon when new Haugean leaders appeared in Bø. Halvor expressed appreciation for a smart and pious layman whom he does not name, but who came to their town and held edifying meetings that impressed Halvor.

About the time of Halvor's confirmation, the town hired a young teacher from the western part of Norway, still known today as the Bible belt of Norway. He knew about the Stavanger mission school and must have recommended it to Halvor, who later yearned to go to the school, but could not find the means. This man also taught them how to read the Bible and spoke to them of spiritual things so movingly that his invitation to read the Bible in Jesus' name brought tears to Halvor's eyes.[7] The teacher had his students sing a song about a black girl, Sarah ("*Den Sorte Sarah*"), who had heard the good news from a missionary and had died believing in Jesus. Halvor said that this song was the seed that would blossom into a clear call to be a missionary. Meanwhile his yearning for education caused his parents to send him to a high school and then a county school (*amtskole*). His thirst for an education became so great that in 1879 he enrolled at Skien's Teacher's School. During his time there he most likely heard the English lawyer, Radcliffe, speaking about China. The entire Rønning family would probably have heard from Halvor on his return home of the great need for missionaries. One night, after hearing a moving lecture on missions, Halvor, walking out in the fields near his home, felt the call to help others come to the knowledge of salvation. Looking up at the stars burning above him, he heard what he believed to be the angels' singing and remembered Jesus' parable in Luke 15: "There is joy in heaven and earth over one sinner's return." He ran to his parents and told them of his experience. It was so powerful a report, according to him, that his oldest sister, Marie, fell to her knees and came to the assurance of salvation at once.[8] Thea writes that after her confirmation she began to hear a similar call to mission.[9]

Because of Halvor's poverty, he could not afford to go to the Stavanger mission high school, which was his dream.[10] In 1883, however, as he was casting about for direction and continuing to struggle with his call to be a missionary, he received a letter from August Weenaas (1835-1924), president and professor at the Hauge Seminary in Red Wing, run by the newly re-constituted Hauge's Synod in America, formerly the Eielsen Synod. Weenaas had left Minneapolis for Norway in 1876 after a stormy conclusion to his time as president of Augsburg Seminary. Upon his return to Norway, he served Bø, Vesteraalen, a parish in the north in the Lofoten region. While there, he had received a call to return to America and lead Red Wing Seminary with the help of Sven Rudolf Gunnersen (1844-1904), his former colleague at Augsburg who had also left the school because he had grown weary of Sverdrup and Oftedal's dominance in the school. In 1879, while considering the call to return to America, Weenaas went to serve the Tinn parish in Telemark. Although Tinn was somewhat remote, the trading town nearest to Tinn was Skien. Weenaas participated in the mission gatherings in the area, about the same time as Halvor was a student in Skien. Halvor's father, Nils Sveinsson (1821-1901), became acquainted with Pastor Ween-

August Weenaas

aas when he lived in Tinn over the summer, building and inspecting roads in the area.[11] Weenaas reported that he traveled so often to mission meetings and Bible studies that his little horse became known in the area as *Missionsbrunen*, (Mission's Brown Horse).[12] Although there is no record in his writings that Weenaas became acquainted with Halvor in Norway, it would have been hard for him not to have noticed at the meetings the tall, handsome student with a passion for mission. Apparently Weenaas regarded the young man highly enough to recruit him as a student at Red Wing, and so he invited him to come.[13] When Halvor received the letter, he answered without hesitation. On June 13, 1883, he left Norway for America in time to begin school that fall semester at the Red Wing Seminary, from which he graduated in 1887. His first call was to three congregations—South Zumbro in Olmsted and Dodge Counties, Markers Hauge Synod congregation just north of Faribault, and Solør, a Hauge Synod congregation near Wanamingo, Minnesota.

When Halvor left for America in 1883, he had been thinking of being a missionary, but China did not appear to be on the front burner. One might have expected a call to Africa, given the song about Black Sarah and the well-known work of Bishop Schreuder. Through the next four years, however, one can see in the Hauge Synod papers a sharp rise in references to the needs in China. Translations of articles from Hudson Taylor's journal, *China's Millions*, were reprinted with increasing frequency. What moved many, especially the women, were the parlous conditions for women in China. The binding of feet and the widespread practice of female infanticide so that women comprised only thirty-five percent of the population, upset many women in the West and moved them to want to help the Chinese women. Hudson Taylor's daughter-in-law, Mary Geraldine Guinness Taylor (1865-1942), wrote many articles in Taylor's periodical, *China's Millions*, begun in 1875, chronicling life in China and Taylor's mission there.[14] Her stories of the suffering of women were almost unbearable, such as the account of a woman who

Geraldine Guinness

had given birth to five girl babies, each one of whom she killed. When the sixth was born, in exasperation, she took it out into the fields, cut it up into many pieces, and spread the remains across the field so as to utterly destroy the spirit of the little girl who wanted so much to be born. Stories such as this, frequently repeated in mission appeals and magazine, both horrified women in the West and gave them the resolve to help China. On September 13, 1886, Taylor issued a call for 100 more missionaries to come to China in 1887. To everyone's astonishment, it happened. Hudson Taylor's call made an impression on world Christians, and those interested in mission could be found even in the smallest towns and farms in Norway.

THEA'S CALL

While Halvor studied at Red Wing, Torbjørg, or later Thea, remained at home in Bø with her other siblings, attending the typical church meetings and Bible studies expected of a young pietist in the small town. All of this encouraged her in her call, an experience she describes as being much the same as her brother Halvor's. These testimonies of finding assurance and then the call to missions are a literary genre with a particular form that describes the same events and insights of Christian's journey in John Bunyan's *Pilgrim's Progress* and in much the same language. The pietists understood their coming to faith in terms of what was called the Order of Salvation and it can be seen in the following summary of Thea's testimony.

She had been born on May 18, 1865, to her parents, Nils Sveinsson and Kjersti Halvorsdatter (1829-1895), in Bø, and baptized ten days later in the old church, dating from the twelfth century, overlooking the valley below it. In her autobiography, published in *Kinamissionæren*, April 15, 1892, she reported that she was sent to school at an early age, and those years were happy for her. In 1880, when she was fifteen, she was confirmed by Pastor Crøger whom both she and Halvor respected as a serious and loving servant of the Lord. Even though she realized her sinfulness and unworthiness, she did not find peace with God at the time. She did, however, rejoice that her three oldest siblings and her parents had been saved. This changed everything at home, but it did not change things for her. This meant that her longings for grace and release from sin continued to trouble her and

Old church in Bø

made her suffer for the next seven years. Then in the spring of 1887 she found peace while reading Psalm 103: "Who forgiveth all thine iniquities, who healeth all thy diseases." Then, she says, the light broke into her troubled soul and she found peace with God. This is a typical description of the order of salvation (*ordo salutis*) which pietists used to describe the process by which the soul came, ultimately, to its heavenly home and life in God. One receives the *call*, then, after some amount of struggle, *illumination*, then *conversion* and *regeneration*, all gifts from God. While she knew she had been elected and called, illumination had not yet occurred so she did not feel what the pietists called "assurance" of salvation. This frequently involved many terrors and struggles as the soul, often a young soul, prepared to make the awesome promises of their confirmation vows, struggling to give over their wills over to the Lord so they could be turned around and utterly changed.

That it did not happen until she was twenty-two years old shows her to have been persistent in her struggles. All this time, however, she was experiencing what she understood to be the "outer call" to be a missionary, a call she pushed aside in the words of many such a testimony: "Send another!"[15] While she struggled with both her inner and outer call, she felt mission work, that is, to bring the needy heathen the Gospel of Jesus Christ, was her "dearest goal and innermost wish."[16] She did not come to these feelings alone. Her brother in Red Wing was very likely sending her letters reporting his own feelings about mission. Just as likely, however, was the steep rise of interest in the China mission in Norway while she was dealing with her own spiritual crisis.

Sofie Reuter Smith

For a bright, but minimally educated young woman like Thea, it must have been thrilling to imagine herself following in the paths of Sofie Reuter and Anna Jacobson. The year that she and her brother Nils emigrated, 1887, was the same year that Hudson Taylor's *China: Its Spiritual Needs and Claims* was translated into Norwegian. Whether Thea read it in Norway or later after her arrival in America we do not know, but Norwegians were most certainly aware of it. When *Kinamissionæren* began publication in 1891, the pamphlet was serialized and included in several numbers of the periodical.

Why she and Nils emigrated, we cannot be sure, except as she noted in a letter home, Norway was poor, and America represented for them a new and better life. They left on June 9, 1887, having received instructions on how to travel from Halvor who had just graduated from Red Wing Seminary and had been ordained as a pastor in the Hauge Synod at its meeting in Lac qui Parle, Minnesota. He had told them to buy tickets to Faribault, but then changed it to Kenyon, too late for them to buy different tickets. This gave them, as Nils said in his account of the trip, a black cloud over their heads while en route. How would they meet up with their brother? America was a huge land.[17] Thea and Nils, along with sixteen others, one their cousin, had traveled together from Bø to Christiania (now Oslo) and stayed there for a few days awaiting their ship, which had sailed from Copenhagen on June 1 and would pick them up on June 2, 1887. The steamship *Geiser,* operated by the Tingvalla line, sailed directly from Christiania to New York, a route emigrants from southern Norway preferred, rather than the trip to Hull, England, and across to Glasgow. While they were waiting in Oslo, Thea wrote a letter home describing their time in the big city, walking around it, marveling at all the sights. They had pictures taken of themselves before they left.[18] "Remember us to God," she concluded.[19]

Their trip to America was rough and stormy. Thea wrote a brief letter describing their journey across the Atlantic, the terrible storm, and their rather minimal accommodations. She shared a room with six girls who became quite seasick and unable even to clean up

Geiser ship

for themselves, which made the journey rather unpleasant. Because it was cold and wet on deck, they could not lie there. Furthermore, the waves were like mountains and the water so rough it looked like a waterfall, foamy and cold. She noted that God apparently did not want to take them yet, otherwise they would have died at sea. Thea marveled that they had not perished in the terrible storms.[20] Otherwise the journey proved uneventful, and their arrival in New York on June 25, 1887, filled them with excitement as well as dread. Neither of them could speak a word of English. With some difficulty, they found the train that would begin their journey to Faribault. Nils records the various mistakes he made on that trip because he could not understand English, nor did he know how much a dollar was worth. In Chicago they changed trains and not long after arrived in Faribault, anxiously wondering how they would make contact with Halvor. After finding a hotel run by Danes whose language they could understand, Nils returned from a foray into the town to find, to his great relief, his brother standing in front of the hotel. Thea reported that, although they knew him immediately, he thought they had changed a lot and could scarcely recognize them, natural enough since he had left them four years before, when Nils was thirteen and Thea sixteen. They went immediately to the parsonage of Pastor Østen Hanson (1836-1898), president of the Hauge Synod, who was serving the Aspelund congregation of the Hauge Synod near Wanamingo, Minnesota. Hanson came from Saude, the neighboring parish to Bø, and they were very likely old acquaintances. This area south of Minneapolis was fertile land, and both Swedes and Norwegians had found it to be good land to farm.

NEWCOMERS IN THE NEW LAND

Aspelund, on the rolling farm land south of Minneapolis, with its green fields stretching out over the miles with no mountains in view, must have seemed to the young farm girl from the mountains and hills of Telemark, Norway, utterly different. The land was richer and far more productive than that of her home. People were spread apart by the requirements of the Homestead Act (1862), which said that to stake a claim one had to live on the quarter section for five years and improve it before the land would be yours. Towns dotted the land in eight mile stretches, about the distance a train's steam engine could travel on a load of coal or wood or a tank of water. By the time she got there, trains were already crisscrossing the state, and she would soon learn to travel on them from one little town to another if necessary. In her first letter home, written July 17, 1887, Thea described their situation living with the Hansons in an utterly new world where there was no state church. The building of churches and synods was completely voluntary. Pastors lived off the contributions and offerings of the parishioners. They also farmed the land, as they had in the old country, but they had no privileges in the New Land. They were, however, probably still afforded respect of a kind from their people who were also happy to be without the established church of Norway which had existed for almost a thousand years. At first it was difficult for the people to realize they needed,

Nils Rønning

voluntarily, to support their pastors with gifts and donations, but they soon adapted and created vigorous congregations and synods in the new land. For Thea this was rather different, and she would note it, with surprise, on occasion in her letters home.

While Nils worked outside on the parsonage farm, she was helping in the house. At first she had been ill, a condition she attributed to the summer heat (something the Scandinavian immigrants at first found unbearable) and the altogether too fine food which she listed with amazement: wheat bread, butter, eggs, meat, bacon, cheese, prim (a kind of cheese), syrup, and so many other things she could scarcely name them all.[21] She regarded Mrs. Østen (Anne) Hanson (1844-1936) as a fine hostess and marveled that she did not seem to be like the pastors' wives in Norway, but was just like any "simple farm wife" out in the country back home.[22] She and Nils stayed with the Hansons for a time in order to become somewhat acquainted with the New Land and begin to learn English, until Halvor was settled in his call to the Solør congregation near Webster. Nils and Torbjørg, as she was still called, moved to be with Halvor when Nils began his schooling at a grammar school in the area. While she was with Mrs. Hanson she learned some English along with other skills that a woman needed to know to keep house in America. For this Thea was most grateful.[23] She had planned to help in the homes of English people in the area who would be eager to hire a servant with her trustworthiness and where she could increase her command of the language. In her letters home she mixed descriptions of their life together with the set pieces of biblical speech, spiritual advice, and prayers typical of the letters pietists wrote each other.

Østen Hanson

In November 1887, in a letter written while she and Nils were awaiting Halvor's return from Olmsted, Thea expressed some weariness with life, something of a constant refrain with her, especially the difficulties of the New Land which she described as "hard" now and then.

Newcomers in the New Land | 31

O that the Lord in his great mercy and grace will help us to struggle and hold out until the last moment when his angels come to take our souls and bear them home to God when the time comes that the body dies and the soul shall leave it.[24]

This longing for the end times, in the language of 1 Thessalonians 4:15-17, was typical of such a person on seeing what she described as the "lusts" and "vanities" of the New Land in which the devil roamed about as a roaring lion. Typical for a person of her spiritual sensibilities, when faced with sin and disobedience around her, she wished for the speedy return of Christ, but added that the Lord was tarrying because so many needed to come to faith and be converted.[25] In this there is a hint of her developing interest in missions, since much of the mission movement of the nineteenth century was driven by the belief that the Lord would return when every soul on earth had heard the good tidings of Jesus. These young people answering Jesus' call to go to the uttermost parts of the earth were going out as much for their love of Jesus as their love of the heathen. They wanted to see Jesus soon. At the close of this letter, Thea bade a hasty goodbye after making a brief complaint about Americans, which is illegible, but at the end of the letter she wrote that she was now a servant in an American home where she had to "suffer severe discipline" since Americans were very difficult to work for, as everything had to be done in haste.[26] It may have been as a servant she discovered the lusts and vanities of an American family, but the copy of the letter, much read and now blackened by too much handling, has obscured her precise complaint.

In a letter written probably in February 1888 from the Hanson's, her mood had lifted, and she assured her family that things were going much better. She wrote with pride that she was now able take the train to Kenyon, where Halvor was, and return to Faribault on her own. Still she valued the Hanson family for the refuge and support they gave her. Almost as though to reassure her family that she was now doing well, she described with relish the Hanson parsonage in terms of the buildings back home: It was almost as large as the Bø parsonage. The hired hand's room was as big as their home in Norway. This was a common piece of rhetoric in the immigrants' letters home: Things were bigger, and life in America was better than in Norway. In response to her mother's wish that she would return to Norway to help there, Thea rejected the idea soundly:

> Nothing will come of that for I am not at all homesick as I am writing and we are doing very well here, so I have no wish to return to poor Norway (*fattige Norge*). I am very glad that I have come here, we are proud that we have become used to the climate and everything gets better with time. One lives only for each day, in America almost every day is like Christmas in Bø. Here is abundance in everything if one will only work. I have $2.50, much more than I would earn in Bø, but I cannot earn more until I can speak English properly, although I understand a great deal now.[27]

Apparently she had overcome her first impressions of America, especially now safe at the Hansons. She was hoping to be able to stay with them so she could help prepare for the large annual synod meeting when many hundreds of people would gather at a church, usually in a rural area where there were no hotels, and need places to stay. Usually they slept in people's homes, sometimes even barns. This would be no problem because of the size of these new buildings, she assured them.[28] As she was learning English and understanding more about the rich and "hard" land where they lived, she was participating in church life. On the last page of the letter she remarked on how cold it could get in Minnesota and then reported on an edifying talk (*oppbygelse*), probably given in January during the mission festivals traditional during the Epiphany season, by a man named Jørgensen, who spoke at the meeting about the mission in Madagascar, which Norwegian and Norwegian-Americans were building at this time, and the need to help these poor folk (*stakkar folk*).[29]

In a letter probably written that same year, Thea described what her life as a servant involved. Working for the Spencer family in Faribault had been an eye opener to her. She seems to have been both attracted and repelled by their riches. In her eyes, they were taken up with nothing but eating, drinking, and clothes, something a Haugean like Thea would describe in biblical terms, such as the rich man in Jesus' parable who says to himself "eat, drink, and be merry." The daughter was married to a dentist who was also living with them. The women, she reported, wore silk dresses every day and everything about them was vain (*Forfengelighed*). The table was covered with a white, wool tablecloth and the silverware was silver, as were the coffee pot, tea pot, and sugar bowl. Then she described the slaughter to her sister, Marie, who as a farmer would have found this interesting.

> The day of slaughter they fry unsalted steaks just five to ten minutes so that the blood runs on the plate, and then they strew salt and pepper on it with butter. That is American and I like it. The food in America is outstanding![30]

We can suppose from her discovery of and delight in rare steak that she had never had such food at home on the farm.

Still, the Americans were strange and different to Thea, and she frequently returned to the Hanson parsonage for comfort and familiarity. The Hansons meant a lot to the Rønning siblings. In his autobiographical statement given for his application to the mission field, Halvor expressed his gratitude for the Hanson's generous sacrifices on their behalf. Just before the Synod meeting in June 1888, one year after they had left Norway, Thea wrote from her brother's home in Faribault (Webster) to her sister Marie to say that Hanson had invited her to come and work for them since Mrs. Hanson had just had a baby and was still not strong enough to handle the housework without help. So she had gotten a reprieve from the Spencers in order to help the Hansons. Halvor had been in Olmsted, and Nils was still in school. Thea gave a picture of the Ladies Aid meeting, reporting a large attendance followed by a prayer meeting that same evening. She then told those at home about other such meetings when Pastor Østen Hanson had been with them for special meetings. The day she was finishing her letter, she said Thorstein Himle (1857-1925), a student at Red Wing (who would leave for China in 1895 as a medical missionary and treat her in her final illness) had come to speak at 7:30 that evening. She had to walk, since no one was there to take her. Thus she had to end the letter quickly in hopes of posting it on her way to church.[31]

Thorstein Himle

The year of 1888 was an exciting one for friends of world mission. The centennial celebration of the missionary movement in London that June had brought missionaries from around the world together in one place, and after the meeting they had traveled across the world on their way back to their respective mission fields, telling one and all of their work and garnering support from their home congregations and churches. Hudson Taylor's trip back to China from this particular conference took him through Canada and the United States. Along the way he spoke many times to thousands of people in order to stir up interest in the China mission. He and Reginald Radcliffe, who had traveled with him, had been overwhelmed by the response he got in America. They spoke at Dwight L. Moody's summer camp in Northfield, Massachusetts, where many decided to become missionaries, and at the large coliseum in Ocean Grove, New Jersey, where still more thousands heard them. Although his biography does not record the other stops he made, the St. Paul and Omaha papers mentioned Taylor's talks in their cities on his way to San Francisco. He first appeared in St. Paul from September 6 to 7 at a large mission conference, speaking at the St. Paul First Baptist Church on September 6 at 3:00 in the afternoon and at House of Hope Presbyterian that evening.[32] At the Baptist church he commissioned some missionaries who were leaving for China. There is no record of the Rønnings marking Taylor's appearance in their state, although they would most certainly have known of him and his mission. Their world was pretty much circumscribed by their Norwegian-American church world—the Hauge Synod in particular—and their English may not have been quite up to such a meeting as yet. Taylor's visits were broadly ecumenical, so it is not that he did not have meetings with Lutherans. When he left St. Paul on his way back to China, he traveled through Omaha where he also spoke at the Kuntze Memorial Lutheran Church on September 10, 1888.[33]

Dwight L. Moody

That December, Thea hosted the Ladies Aid. In the previous letter she had said that they had between sixty and seventy people in attendance at a prior meeting of the aid and they had collected over seven dollars for mission.[34] Unfortunately she does not say where it was to be sent. Her letter, however, does give evidence of the growing interest in mission in the new settlements. She did not mention that she had any interest in going herself. That would take some time, but one can sense from the letters that, as she was getting settled in America and taking part in church life with her brothers, she was hearing more and more about missions, a concern of her brothers' colleagues and fellow students, as well as the topic of the Ladies Aids.

One can also feel that the Hauge Synod pastors were becoming especially aware of the urgent needs in China through the work of several Norwegians who had been touched by the work of Hudson Taylor. The idea of a China mission began to burn more fervently in the pastors and members of the Hauge Synod as they started to push for the church to establish a mission to China. Nowhere among Norwegian-Americans would the interest be more intense than in the Ladies Aids of the Hauge Synod at the time.

LADIES AIDS AND MISSIONS

Most Norwegian-American women's missionary societies of the late nineteenth century traced their organization back to Norway and the work of Mrs. Gustava Kielland (1800-1889). When she gathered a group of women to support the mission work of the Norwegian Mission Society (*Norsk Misjons selskap*), she realized quickly they needed to have a clear sense of their mission and rules for the group, if only a "few and simple."[35] On the appointed day they would meet, without forsaking their household duties, and work as long as they could. Each meeting they contributed two shillings, or whatever they could, to the treasury. When the sheep were sheared in the spring and fall, each would bring some wool to the meeting. This they would card and spin into yarn which they would knit into usable clothing for the mission. Later it was decided, as a group grew larger, that the meetings, which as a rule had been at the parsonage, could be held at any other home, if one or another of the group so wished. Wherever the meeting was to be held, the group would be served coffee and sandwiches. It was strictly forbidden to serve anything more or finer.

In her memoirs, Mrs. Kielland noted that their work was very successful and met with her husband's approval, though not all men were so approving. Constant fears were expressed that the meetings, unless strictly controlled, would turn into mere gossip and eating societies, a fear expressed time and time again in America when the subject of women's societies was broached to the male leadership. When the immigrant women arrived they must have noticed the flourishing women's groups

Gustava Kielland

of their Yankee neighbors, all devoted to missions as well as local improvements in the congregation and locale.

Most likely, the first Ladies Aids formed by Norwegian-American women in this country started about 1858 when Diderikke Ottesen Brandt (1827-1885) gathered some women together to support the Norwegian students who were attending Concordia Seminary in St. Louis. Mrs. Brandt, a formidable woman concerned for the education of both men and women in the community, was said to have attended a school for girls in Christiansfeld, North Schleswig, now Denmark, owned by the Moravian Brethren. There she had studied German, English, music, and the arts necessary for a lady: fine hand work and crafts. After her confirmation in Sande, Norway, where her father, Realf Ottesen, was pastor, she is said to have taken a finishing tour of Denmark, Germany, Holland, and England. Legend has it that she was presented at court to Oscar I, king of Norway and Sweden. With experiences like this it is no wonder that she would be a leader of the women in the Norwegian Synod when she arrived. As the new bride of Pastor Nils Olsen Brandt (1824-1921) in 1856, who was serving the parish in Rock River, Wisconsin, she organized the women into small groups to sew for the young students at Concordia Seminary where the Norwegian Synod seminary students were studying until such time as the Norwegians could build their own school. She very likely had learned to do this in her student days in Denmark, as well as from the example of Mrs. Kielland in Norway. It is also possible that as an avid student of the American scene—she is said to have attended a girls' school in Wisconsin to learn to speak and write English better—she adapted her Norwegian tradition to the frontier where the American Ladies Aids had become a well-developed social form.

Diderikke Ottesen Brandt

It was not until after the Civil War, as more and more immigrant women arrived in this country and the older settlements were more established, that Ladies Aids became regular organizations in the Norwegian-American Lutheran congregations. When they organized, many recalled the work of their foremother Mrs. Kielland and the rules she had suggested for their organization and gatherings. Careful to allay suspicions among the men that they were merely gossip and eating societies, they wrote their constitutions with this criticism in mind. Generally they made their first obligation the local congregation—paying off its debt, buying a bell, or furnishing the church. After that, they committed themselves to helping the poor and needy in their own midst. Then they agreed to work for missions in more distant lands. This hierarchy of purposes obtained well into the twentieth century and served to organize the work of the women.

Ladies Aid Meeting at Ole Groven's home

From the first, missions had been fundamental to their reason for gathering, though it would be foolish to deny that part of their reason for gathering was social. They were isolated from each other and caught in an endless round of daily labor which could be crushing to the hardiest souls. Most women brought handiwork which they either planned to sell at a bazaar or send to the mission they had chosen to support. One Ladies Aid historian wrote that their meetings generally were once a month and lasted all day. Their usual attire was calico dresses with white aprons. The day of the meetings they could be seen walking along the country roads from early in the morning, on their way to the farm house where the meeting was going to be. Sometimes farmers would pick them up in their lumber wagons and, as the wagons approached the house where the aid was being held, they would be carrying several women and children. Frequently, the entire family would come along to the meeting, and every one of them would partake of the special food prepared for the day. Sometimes the aids included men, as it was thought women had no organizational skills, or sometimes the pastors harbored the suspicion on the basis of Paul's letter to the Corinthians that women should not lead a public meeting. Thea and Halvor Rønning participated in these societies along with their compatriots in the new land. The history of Solør congregation during Halvor Rønning's time as pastor gives us a picture of what the first meetings looked like when the women started to organize their aids. At the first meeting, the congregational history reports, the first president was a man, as was the treasurer. One man moved that two kinds of cake be served. Another man suggested rather timidly that one kind of sandwich and one kind of cake be served. This was too much for Rev. Rønning. Somewhat sarcastically he asked "Is this a Ladies Aid or a man's society?"[36]

One aid historian reported what a typical Ladies Aids gathering included: The day began at 10:00 with lemonade and cookies or maybe a fine brewed wine and cake. The dinner, or *middag*, was followed in the late afternoon by coffee and cake which concluded the gathering. Preachers watched these events with suspicion and were quick to point out when they were becoming too venal. Pastor Jørgen Nelson Sandven (1855-1900), a Hauge Synod pastor with a long commitment to the China mission, scolded the Ladies Aid in his congregation for eating too much. Soon the group passed a rule that they would not begin with morning coffee, but with the dinner, a large meal served about 2:00 in the afternoon. This still seemed excessive for Sandven because it consisted, generally, of three kinds of meat, lutefisk, vegetables, salad, potatoes, cake, and cookies. According to the report, Sandven and his wife continued their attack, suggesting that the women eat dinner before they came to the meeting and only expect coffee and dessert at the meeting. The desserts, of course, were to be kept simple.[37]

Looking back at Gustava Kielland's discussion of what they had done in their group to allay such suspicions, one can see a constant effort on the part of the women not to offend their men folk. Even then, what the women were up to in their meetings caused the men discomfort. One pastor was said to have come to a meeting of the pastors' wives and taken his wife by the ear, saying, "There are enough socks to darn at home!" So it is not surprising that when the women founded their groups, they were careful to make certain that their main duties at home were not neglected in favor of the aid.

This question of the priority of purposes often rankled, even within the women's group. Mrs. Hjalmar (Caroline) Madland (1888-1955), a pastor's wife born in Inwood, Iowa, near Canton, South Dakota, wrote about her mother, clearly a supporter of the China mission, who had worked hard in the Our Savior's Ladies Aids, both the Tabitha and Lydia Circles, all through her life. Having come from the parish of Gustava Kielland in Vang, she had some decided opinions about the purposes of such meetings.

> In spite of many difficulties and hardships, they (the women) organized a Ladies Aid of which my mother was an active member. After some years when the pioneers had built their first church the Ladies Aid was called to finance the cost of a church bell. Then a controversy arose, because most of the members wanted to drop the work for mission and work only for the church bell. This my mother resented. She wanted to work for both. But then as now, the majority ruled. The church bell became the only project of the aid. Therefore, Mother organized another aid for the women who were not members of the first aid. In this aid the work for mission carried on, consisted of supporting a native missionary in China. Mother kept her membership in both aids until some years later the two aids merged.[38]

By the 1880s, Norwegian-American Lutheran were well aware of the needs around the world, though they had not, as yet, a foreign mission operation of their own. The immigrants, still loyal to their home churches, tended to send their mission support money back to Norway. Even as they expressed their support in this way, they were learning about other missions and other fields of mission enterprise from the Norwegian and Norwegian-American press. The names of the great pioneer missionaries, William Carey in India, Adoniram Judson in Burma, and Hudson Taylor in Chian appeared as frequently in the Norwegian religious press as they did in the American press. Taylor's impact on the Scandinavian churches was clear in the two women from Norway, Sophie Reuter and Anna Jacobson. Reuter and Jacobson left for China and arrived in

Stanley Smith

Shanghai on March 18, 1885. Their story brought many thousands to an interest in and commitment to the China mission as well. Reuter was to marry Stanley Smith, one of the most famous missionaries to China. Smith had been one of the Cambridge Seven Stars who over their years at Cambridge converted and gained an interest in China by reading Taylor's book *China's Spiritual Need and Claims*.[39]

Already by the first part of the 1880s, Ladies Aids, although not yet national organizations, were writing to the church leaders and asking where they should send the money they had gathered for missions in their various endeavors. In his 1883 report to the Hauge Synod, President Arne Boyum (1833-1913) told the annual meeting that when such women asked him where and how to send their gifts to mission, he replied that they should divide it equally among the various causes they had, both at home and elsewhere.[40] Another spark for missions in the church, especially among the women of the Hauge Synod and Conference, was the visit, in the spring of 1884, of Missionary Christian Doederlein Borchgrevink (1841-1919) to the Midwest. He had given the Norwegian mission in Madagascar visibility, and his work was storied among the Norwegians both in Norway and America. It was not surprising that the Norwegian-Americans in 1887, through the Conference, sent out its first missionary to Madagascar, Johan Peter Hogstad (1858-1911). Many congregations, led by their Ladies Aids, feted Borchgrevink in his visits to the Norwegian Lutheran congregations in the Midwest.

Every month *Budbæreren* published reports from various Ladies Aids about their organizations, especially their constitutions, whose by-laws generally included something similar to the three purposes of the Porter, Wisconsin, Ladies Aid: 1) to gather funds for the upkeep of the church, 2) to aid and promote Christian education in the congregation, 3) to support home and foreign missions. Others would report, for example, how much money they had raised, such as: the "Hope Ladies Aid had had an auction in which they raised $60.84, $50 of which was loaned to a worthy cause in the congregation."[41] In Roland, Iowa, the Salem Ladies Aid had sent its first collection to the Mission high school in Stavanger. In 1886, it devoted one-half of its offering to foreign missions, the other half to inner mission and Jewish mission. The stories of missionaries stoked the flames of their causes.

Thus, the importance of articles about missionaries such as Miss Sofie Reuter Smith, who was reputed to have been a great preacher, something the women thinking of missions and perhaps feeling a call to public ministry found encouraging, maybe even tantalizing. *China's Millions,* the magazine of the China Inland Mission, printed in its October 26, 1887, issue, the *Diary of Miss Reuter* which did much to raise the awareness of Scandinavians of the mission to China. Some months later, Benjamin Bagnall (1844-1900), an American Presbyterian and secretary of the American Bible Society, wrote a letter concerning the work of the two Norwegian women missionaries, giving a clear picture of their work and effect in China.

Hsiu-chi Cheng, Sofie Reuter, and Anna Jakobsen

> At Hoh-chan, Misses Reuter and Jakobsen are much encouraged, and are very happy in their work. They are visited by large numbers of women, many of whom belong to the middle and upper classes, and they are able to enter the homes of many respectable families. They are much loved by the Christians.[42]

Sometime later, the same magazine reported that Miss Reuter was like a magnet thrown among needles: "the women rose *en masse* to hear her."[43] At the end of the article on Miss Reuter, an announcement appeared saying that for a penny, one could obtain a copy of Miss Reuter's diary and some letters in a volume entitled, *Consecration and Blessing*.[44] That work stirred up interest in Nor-

Ladies Aids and Missions | 43

way and Sweden as well as in the American religious press. By now Taylor's book, *China's Spiritual Need and Claims,* had been printed in several of the Norwegian and Norwegian-American periodicals.

By the mid-1880s, church leadership in every Protestant denomination watched these funds being directed to causes the women chose, and fretted the money did not always end up in the places they wanted it to go. There is a telling note in the Norwegian Danish Augustana Synod's *Luthersk Kirketidende* from Pastor Iver Christian Larson Hatlestad (1853-1909) that "the women's organizations should also help the schools "as well as missions.[45] President Herman Preus (1826-1894) of the Norwegian Synod, who had opposed the organization of any ladies organization in Spring Prairie and only relented after his wife died in 1880, wrote a similar letter to the churches in the *Evangelisk Luthersk Tidende,*

Herman A. Preus

the paper of the Norwegian Synod. "To the Synod Pastors and Congregations," he wrote, "The Professor's Fund is overdrawn! I would ask our many women's groups to come to the help of the Synod, if possible, and send immediately money to the fund."[46] The issue seemed to have become a pressing one for many, so much so that the General Assembly of an Inter-Synodical Mission group at its fourth general assembly in Wittenberg, Wisconsin, resolved that

> Whether the congregation be large or small, rich or poor, old or newly organized, whether it has a church building or not, the cause of mission should be a common task for the entire congregation as much as the support of the pastor and the instruction of the children."[47]

From this brief glimpse we can see that the cause of women missionaries still created some difficulties with the church mission boards, run exclusively by men, until the centennial conference on world missions in London, June 1888. The conference made some significant contributions to the debate. Just before this the Norwegian Mission Society had discussed the question of women being sent out as missionaries:

The thought is new and not much debated which means that not much has been decided about it. The Society did note that young women were beginning to train as deaconesses, nurses, Bible teachers—the case is before the mission board and their decision will have great consequence when it is taken up in the summer.[48]

The London meeting, although criticized for its failures, did treat the topic seriously. Many male missionary leaders had strong responses to what they learned. Although women had been serving as missionaries most of the century, not every church body or mission society had agreed it was a good thing. An editorial in the *Missionary Review of the World* argued that women were important in the history of the church because of their high moral character. They could say from their own experience of other cultures and religions that it was largely Christianity that had raised the condition of women.[49]

The official Norwegian observer at the conference, Lars Dahle (1843-1925), who had just left his impressive work in Madagascar to return to serve as the general secretary of the Norwegian Mission Society (*Det Norske Misjonsselskap*), noted that many women at the conference spoke to *mixed* groups of men and women, a practice which seemed to surprise him. The Board of the Norwegian Mission Society at that time had already been grappling with the issue of women being sent out on their own to do direct mission work. Although they had not come to a decision on the matter of single women missionaries yet, Norwegian-American Lutherans were also part of the ferment about the matter. The case was discussed widely in the mission magazines and journals during the summer of 1888. *Lutheraneren*, the paper of the Norwegian Danish Conference edited by Georg Sverdrup, reported that even if the idea was new it did know that

Lars Dahle

Ladies Aids and Missions | 45

a young woman was becoming a deaconess in order to be a teacher and nurse on a mission field. In a report on the conference in London, the writer noted that many different causes were represented. Of fifty-two societies represented from the USA, twenty were women's organizations. There were seven from England, six from Canada, eighteen from Europe, and many of those women spoke at the meeting, the reporter noted.[50] That it was an issue for Norwegians on both sides of the ocean is not difficult to understand. Han Nielsen Hauge had empowered women to be leaders and even preach if their preaching could be proven to be faithful to Scripture; at the same time, he had been attacked by many of his followers for not following the word of God on the issue of women's leadership. His regiment of women, however, followed him and did much good for the awakening in Norway, none more effective than Berte Canutte Aarflot (1795-1869), whose hymns and letters of spiritual comfort revealed her to be a much beloved *Sjælesorger* (carer for souls) to many Norwegians who sought out her counsel in their own spiritual journeys.

As reports on the London Conference were disseminated throughout the world in many different mission magazines, it became clear how important women were to the mission effort. The conference had tried to honor that fact even in its schedule. Although most of the women were wives of missionaries and mission executives, the women in and of themselves did make an impact. "Women's work" was an assigned topic for two of the regular sessions for all of the delegates, men and women. One of the evening lectures open to the public dealt with the topic, and there were meetings exclusively for the "ladies." Canadian Baptist Hannah Maria Norrise-Armstrong addressed a plenary session. Women did speak at, if not to, public meetings, and some were called upon for responses at various lunches and breakfasts. The morning sessions for women had been scheduled to meet in the Annex of Exeter Hall where the event took place. The hall, however, held only two-hundred and fifty and was too small, so it was necessary to adjourn to a larger hall to accommodate the crowd.[51]

One of the most controversial sessions was the paper by Dr. Murdoch of the American Baptist Union, "The Relation of Woman's Boards to the General Boards." This addressed what had been a troublesome issue for both the women's groups and the church executives who wanted control of the money the women were raising.

> While he placed great estimate on woman's work, he advocated that all female agencies should abide by the rules of and be governed by the policies of the General Board; that it would be better for both and have a better effect on the natives when women recognized the headship of man in ordering the affairs of the Church of God, remembering that "Adam was the head.[52]

The sentiments of the "brave" doctor, as the report referred to him, were not highly regarded by many of the women there, one of whom—an American—remarked on hearing it, "All Buncomb!"[53] One can see this same concern in the pastors of the Norwegian-American Lutheran churches who had begun to envy the power of women to raise money. They wanted control of all the money they saw being gathered from the women. One woman, president of one of the more successful societies, said "she would rejoice to see their work merged into one, for the burden and responsibility were great on women alone."[54] If that were the case, however, the women who raised the money should have a place on the committees that spent the money. This was not about to happen.

Some of the papers, which Lars Dahle thought were too short, only twenty minutes long, dealt with the history of women as missionaries, with others on what kind of training a woman should have before going. It was generally agreed that women should have three lines of study in preparation for their work: 1) Bible, 2) methods of teaching the Bible, and 3) nursing, teaching, or medicine. The *Missionary Review of the World* reprinted a paper by Mrs. Lucy Rider Meyer laying out the case for special training for women to teach the Bible, which was necessary if they were to be effective missionaries:

> There is a difference between men and women's work, but if men called of God to a special work need a special training for that work, do not also women, called of God to their special work, need a special training for that work?[55]

The conference did not resolve the question, nor could it stop the growing flood of women missionaries going to the farthest reaches of the globe. Women had been serving on the mission fields since the early part of the century, and the men knew they needed them to get access to the homes where the mothers could do the most effective mission work. No matter what a church executive might say, people such as Hudson Taylor and others had already asked for women to come, and some of their most effective missionaries had been women.

This is also important for understanding why Thea could think of going as a single woman missionary to China. Even though many men did not approve of women in teaching roles in the church or society, they could not deny that women evangelized women best, and many church leaders understood quickly that evangelizing women was the best way to get to the entire family. Thus, women vital to mission work, and single women especially, could be called to go to the uttermost parts of the world even though it caused the mission boards some theological anguish. There is little to suggest that the Norwegian-American women differed in any significant way in their attitudes from their Yankee peers who were also going to school, receiving educations, and entering a variety of vocations hitherto closed to them. Norwegian-Americans responded favorably to efforts to educate young women at St. Olaf College, and the Deaconess Movement was beginning to flower at the time. Becoming a missionary and going off to a foreign land was a new career option for women who may not have found marriage either possible or desirable. In choosing this vocation they were simply following the logic of their sisters in the Ladies Aids who chose to support missionaries to women in distant lands who needed to hear the gospel. Through their Ladies Aids they could raise money, spend it on their own projects, and find solace in each other, even as they supported the works of the larger church.

THE O. S. NESTEGAARD BROTHERS

Into this world came a young man, Ole Syversen Nestegaard (1860-1937), from Norway, the first male missionary from Norway to China. Nestegaard, whose emotional and mental stability appear at this distance to have been somewhat questionable, and whose peripatetic adventures in a day without airplanes are still astonishing, issued a clarion call to his people in Norway and America to go to China. His biography reveals a restless man driven to distraction by the call of China's millions.[56] The son of a farmer in the Hoel Parish in Hallingdal, Ole had no interest in the farm, which his father was intending to divide among his many sons, another of whom was also named Ole Syversen Nestegaard (the younger), who also had a passion for the China mission.

After confirmation, he attended the grammar school in Aal and then attended the diocese school there in 1879. His interest in missions grew apace. When he heard that Lars Skrefsrud (1840-1910) of the Santal Mission in India was going to speak in Drammen, he walked nearly 200 kilometers to Bragernæs church to hear the missionary. Many young people in Norway at the time, even the painter Edvard Munch, admired Skrefsrud, who was a hero to them for his story of being imprisoned for an infraction of the law, converting in jail, learning many languages, plus being a strong and impressive man. On hearing Skrefsrud, Nestegaard the elder began an itinerant preaching mission with Iver Lien, another layman he knew. Soon he enrolled in Pastor Johan Storjohann's

Ole Syversen Nestegaard the elder

(1832-1914) school, Luther Seminary (*Lutherseminariet*) in Oslo, which had been established to prepare pastors for the American and Australian Norwegian churches. While there he saw a flyer from Pastor Per A. Ahlberg of the Mission school in Örebro, Sweden.[57] Despite his financial exigencies, Nestegaard enrolled there for three terms, though economic conditions were so meager the students barely had enough to eat. Nestegaard received good reports from the school for his work, especially his linguistic talents. When he returned to Norway he again took up lay preaching in the Sunmøre regions, where his work helped spark an awakening in Sundfjord.

Although he was accepted provisionally by Stavanger's mission school, he did not make the grade. Looking for something to further his training for mission work, he heard from a sailor that there was a missionary training home in London, Pastor Baxter's mission school, run by a Miss Hedenström. He soon appeared at the school where he took up the study of English and discovered to his delight that the offices for Taylor's China Inland Mission were in the neighborhood. He took the opportunity to become acquainted with Taylor's staff. After that he returned to Norway where he traveled throughout the country gathering money for his mission and speaking about the need in China. It was probably during this time that both Halvor and Thea heard him or at least heard about him. At the end of 1887, around Christmas, Nestegaard returned to London. There he won permission to travel with some of Taylor's missionaries to China, although he was not accepted as one of Taylor's missionaries for reasons that remain murky. From the reports on the reaction of mission boards and church judicatories to his requests for ordination or authorization, it appears he was regarded with suspicion. The association with Taylor, however, was for him the chance of a lifetime.

In 1888, he arrived in Ganjing, China, a city on the Yangzi, about 150 miles west of Nanjing, Although it is said that he was not a member of the China Inland Mission (CIM) group, he does appear, somewhat tacked on, in a picture of 100 missionaries who went to China in answer to Taylor's call for new missionaries. Nestegaard enrolled at the school of the CIM where he studied the Chinese language and culture. His letters home to Norway and America described China's geography, culture, religions, and its needs of challenging both young men and women to answer the call to come.[58] His letters awakened a good bit of interest among Norwegian-Americans, especially among the Haugeans and the Conference. Among many other influences, Nestegaard's place in the call of the young American church to establish a mission in China was probably the most immediate and effective. What he wrote to the American churches, published in *Lutheraneren* and *Bud-*

One hundred missionaries. Nestegaard is at bottom right.

bæreren, about conditions in China evoked much response. The last day of a General Assembly meeting of the Hauge Synod in Estherville, Iowa, September 12, 1889, was devoted to the China mission and letters from Nestegaard were read and discussed.[59] The farmer

Daniel Nelson was moved to sell his farm and prepared to leave for China after hearing them, though it must be added that Nelson had been burdened for China ever since he had visited there as a sailor on a Norwegian ship. Once again one wonders whether any in the group went to the July meetings at the Mahtomedi, Minnesota, Chautauqua series where Hudson Taylor had appeared with one of the Seven Stars, Charles T. Studd (1860-1931). Studd, the son of a wealthy English family and something of a celebrity of the day, had been a world famous cricket player. His conversion and devotion to mission was a draw for most people around the world. His travels in America with Taylor drew thousands to hear them speak on the need in China. During these years, Taylor traveled widely to whip up enthusiasm for the mission. However it happened, the topic of the China Mission was also having an impact on the immigrants, both from their homelands, as well as the new land.

Daniel and Anna Nelson

Nestegaard's letters were like spark on gasoline. Ever since 1886 when the Hauge Synod, at its quarterly meeting in Radcliffe, Iowa, on October 7 through 10, had gone on record urging that the Synod should do more for mission, the pressure within the Synod grew greater and greater. Even before the group was founded, the concern for the women of China and finding women to go to China was a major priority of the group. Nestegaard never failed to mention the need for women missionaries.[60] On July 12, 1888, Østby sent an appeal from Taylor's daughter-in-law, Miss Guinness, to the church paper *Lutheraneren*, pleading with the American churches to send missionaries, especially women. "The cry of women around me is terrible," she wrote. "All these unlucky women cry as one to the heart of God."[61] The challenge Hudson Taylor issued in the December 1889 issue of *China's Millions* to send 1000 missionaries from Europe and North America added more urgency. It was his estimate that with such numbers in five years they could reach all 250,000,000 Chinese with the gospel. Although it is not quite clear that the Norwegian-Americans heard much about it, the visit of Hudson Taylor to Scandinavia in 1889 created a huge sensation. Taylor could not believe the massive numbers who came to hear him speak; over 5000 heard him in Stockholm. People would travel for days to hear him, and from these numbers it is natural to imagine some who would hear the call to be missionaries in China. In fact, by the next year when he and his wife and daughter-in-law were in Shanghai, a Swedish man came to the CIM headquarters there and announced that there were thirty-five more behind him. The Taylors were stunned, although Taylor himself had grown accustomed to miracles like this. These stories created a buzz and served to further energize the Hauge Synod pastors who were beginning to push the church to do something quickly. A letter from Miss Guinness to all Christians recounting the death of a young Chinese girl from opium in the arms of a missionary appeared in the February 22, 1890, *Lutheraneren*, and must have fueled the fire even more.[62]

Nestegaard the younger

Although Nestegaard had been in China in August 1889, *Lutheraneren* announced that he and Sigvald Netland (1868-1896) would be in Minneapolis for the 1890 annual meeting of the Hauge Synod. Netland, from Songdal near Kristiansand, had also been moved by the need in China and had actually gone to England in 1889 to attend the Baxter Training Home in London which trained missionaries. Somewhere, maybe at the Baxter school, he had met one of the Nestegaards. In 1890, Netland immigrated to a farm near Crookston, Minnesota, where the younger Nestegaard is said to have come as a fifteen year old.[63] Both of the brothers appeared at the forty-fifth annual convention, June 4 through 11, 1890, at the Hauge Norwegian Evangelical Lutheran congregation in Jackson, Minnesota. During that meeting, a group of Hauge Synod ministers and lay people tried to bring to the floor the matter of establishing immediately a mission that would send missionaries to China. Nestegaard, who had traveled from San Francisco to meet his brother, O. S. Nestegaard the younger, in Crookston, Minnesota, was there with Sigvald Netland, both of whom were about to leave for China. They spoke to the gathering about China. Their proposal, made with the support of Pastor Ole A. Østby, to send missionaries to China was referred to a committee. The supporters of a China mission organization in the synod thought this was a tactic of delay and ultimately a lack of concern for mission.

While it might not be correct to say it was a lack of concern, it was perhaps the move of an older, wiser man. Østen Hanson, who served as president of the synod during the most turbulent years of Norwegian-American church life, 1887-1893, must have been exhausted by the idea of taking up another organizational burden. His energies had been spent finding the money to support the Red Wing Seminary, trying to keep it and the synod going, wondering whether or not to join the United Church which was forming during this time, alongside calls for a common hymnal among all the Norwegian-American churches. The synod finally refused to participate in the negotiations which resulted in the newly established United Church, with which it had cordial relations. At the time of this effort he was sixty-four, and had a three year old at home. From this vantage point it looks like he was exhausted and did not have the energy to proceed.

Ole A. Østby

The younger pastors were clearly chafing to get going. Pastor Ole A. Østby (1862-1931), one of the young Turks in the synod, wrote a letter and worked to organize an independent society for the China mission after Hanson, in his capacity as president, refused to recognize him at the meeting. A good number of those wanting faster action decided to bolt the convention and meet in a field beside the church where the convention was being held that year, mimicking the Haystack Oath of the Seven at Williams College. Led by Pastor Anders Olsen Oppegaard (1841-1919) and Østby, who were to become leading lights in the China Mission Society, they resolved to establish a China mission sooner than the Hauge Synod felt they could. They formed a society, the Norwegian Evangelical Lutheran China Mission Society in America (*Den norsk-evangelisk Lutherske Kinamissionsforening*). Oppegaard was voted president, Østby treasurer, and Halvor Rønning secretary. Although the organization consisted mostly of Hauge Synod people, members of the United Norwegian Lutheran Church in America (*Den Forenede Norsk Lutherske Kirke i Amerika*), formed in 1890, were also invited to be a part of the group. Østby became the editor of the new periodical, *Kinamissionæren*, and by 1891 he was publishing the monthly paper from Madison, Minnesota, on the new society's work.

Until then Østby had used both the papers of the United Church (*Lutheraneren*) and the Hauge Synod (*Budbæreren*) to get the news out. The August 2, 1890, edition of *Lutheraneren* included another appeal from Østby. "Come to China," he said, "pastors, laymen, men and women." And then he appealed to the women's organizations to sponsor a missionary.[64] His new magazine would frequently appeal to women's groups to get behind the cause, and he reported on their activities in order to get the word out and spark the movement even more. At the same time as the society was being founded, a revival had broken out in the Radcliffe, Iowa, area. Missions would have been high on the list of concerns of the revival as well. Daniel Nelson had already left for China, although the China Mission Society had not been around to support him. The quick establishment of the society was met with skepticism in the Norwegian Synod's paper, *Evangelisk Luthersk Kirketidende,* in its own August 2, 1890, issue. It viewed with somewhat jaundiced eyes the announcement that the Hauge Synod and the China Mission Society were working to establish a mission, calling it premature. The Norwegian Synod, the editor allowed, also would like to establish a mission in China, but the people they called would have to be very well-educated people and that would take time.[65]

The first meeting of the China Mission Society was held at the Aspelund congregation on August 25 to 30, 1890. Thea wrote home to Norway on August 28, 1890, telling about the meeting and Nestegaard's visit with them. Halvor was at Østen Hanson's church for a meeting on the mission in China with Nestegaard, whom Thea reported would be ordained at that meeting. One wonders from this remark whether or not her family back home in Norway knew of him. It would not be surprising if they did, given Nestegaard's reputation in Scandinavia. Here she remarked on the situation in China and mentioned for the first time that Halvor was feeling called to go to China as well, but not before the next spring. The situation of the poor Chinese was a call to her as well. "We should do more for them than we have," she commented.[66] One can hear in this rather wistful sentence something of a longing to also answer the call to go. On August 31, 1890, Hanson ordained Nestegaard the elder at Aspelund, and he immediately returned to Norway where he was met with suspicion by the church authorities there. Lars Dahle found that Nestegaard had not fully obeyed the instructions of Hudson Taylor and felt that he was something of an

Rønning (third from left) and Nestegaard (fourth from left) with a family in Aspelund.

untrustworthy representative of the church. After much strife and no real resolution to the conflict, Nestegaard continued his travels through Norway and Denmark, seeking to awaken more interest in the China mission.

After the decision to found the China Mission Society during the summer of 1890, Ole S. Nestegaard the younger and Sigvald Netland traveled through the Upper Midwest raising interest in the Norwegian China mission. Support increased as they went about the countryside. There are records in history after history of Ladies Aids whose support for mission increased substantially in those years simply because of the personal contact these people made with them. By January 1891, Østby had found the wherewithal to publish the first issue of *Kinamissionæren.* Later, when it grew more established, its cover would feature a Chinese pagoda with Chinese standing about it in darkness. To the right, in the light, is a typical Midwestern country church with Chinese people entering into it.

Sigvald Netland

In the first issue, Pastor O. A. Oppegaard, president of the society, reported on the founding meeting of the society and expressed his gratitude that Pastor H. N. Rønning and his sister, Thea, had agreed to take the call to China. Halvor prepared to resign his call to the Solør congregation to get ready for their departure in the not too distant future. There are no letters extant from Thea at this time, so we are not able to trace her growing awareness of a call, but we know from her brief autobiography, the story of her call to be a missionary, published in the magazine, that she had felt called to be a missionary, but was resisting it. Oppegaard had obviously spoken with the brother and sister and had discerned her call as well as Halvor's. By now Netland had arrived in China and had written a letter from Wuchang to the magazine about the challenges there. Once again the need to have women in the mission was clear to them all. Oppegaard went on to say that if any of the readers, men or women, wanted to go to China, they should send him an autobiography and a recommendation from the nearest Lutheran pastor.[67] The March 14 edition of *Budbæreren* contained a letter to the Hauge Synod congregations from Østby saying that the society was working to found a mission, and they needed a leader who understood the work in this country and another in China who understood the work there. "We will send our own tried and true men and women to work in the mission," he said.⁶⁸

The spring of 1891 brought devastating floods and famine to China. The March 15 edition of *Kinamissionæren* reported that the need in China was almost indescribable. The people, in their hunger, were forced to eat grass. On April 1, 1891, the journal published a sober analysis of Chinese civilization, almost as though it felt that the negative reports on China up to that time had been too much. The article described the ancient civilization, which was older than Socrates or Moses, praising the Chinese for their fine, though elitist, educational system. The pride of the Chinese in their civilization caused problems for the missionaries, the article admitted, but this was no reason to criticize the missionaries. The religion of China was seen to be one of the reasons for its downfall. "In China it is easier to find a god than a human being," the article concluded, going on to speak with passion about the position of women within the culture. Chinese religion and culture allowed women no souls, it bound their feet, and girl babies were frequently killed or sold into slavery.⁶⁹ Undoubtedly these reports were believed, because they came directly from writers whom the subscribers had come to know through their personal appearances as well as their letters. They stirred up a great deal of interest and concern among both Hauge Synod members and Ladies Aids throughout the Upper Midwest. who followed the news that the younger Nestegaard and Netland in Wuchang, across the river from Daniel Nelson and his family in Hankow, had just rented a native house there.

As the summer began, it was time for the annual meeting of the Hauge Synod. Hosted by congregations around Minnesota and Iowa, people came from all the congregations after the spring planting and before haying, to meet as a church body and debate issues and enjoy each other's company, almost like family. It was with anticipation that the members of the synod gathered on June 3, 1891, at the Arendahl church near Rushford, Minnesota, near the beautiful Mississippi Valley with its bluffs towering over the Rush River. As the meeting went on, so many people came they had to remove the church windows so people could hear what was going on inside. People were now ready to support the mission work of

Thea and Halvor Rønning. After some discussion, the synod passed a resolution to share the support of the Rønnings with the China Mission Society. Then both Halvor and Thea spoke, which was a bit of a stretch for some of the people in the group who were a bit worried about women addressing a mixed group in church, given the words of St. Paul. Thea stressed in her speech that they were going to China to proclaim the living God. She directed her speech to the women, thanking them for their support and the good resources available to them in America. She hoped they would uphold them in prayer. The Rønning speeches were said by those who attended to be the most gripping of all the speeches given at the convention. With that the group sang the traditional mission hymn by Wexels, "O Happy Day When We Shall Stand" (*"O Tænk når engang vi samles skal"*). As they prepared to leave, they gathered for a picture surrounding the church, maybe because they were so proud of what they had done. As they bade each other good bye, people remarked on the Rønning speeches during the meeting.[70] They had come to know the two young people and would never forget the impression they made at this meeting. This would be just one more connection with the missionaries that would help them later when they wrote home from China telling of their work there.

Thea and Halvor Rønning

By this time the increasing suspicions regarding Nestegaard the elder made it necessary for Hanson to defend his ordination of Nestegaard the previous August. He was careful to say that he had agreed to do so only after the church council had granted him permission. All had been done in order, he wrote. These suspicions continued in the churches after the letter written by Lars Dahle of the Norwegian Mission Society announcing to potential support-

The O. S. Nestegaard Brothers | 59

ers of Nestegaard that they should not give any money to him, but rather send it directly to the society which would then distribute it as they thought proper. As the Rønnings were making preparations to leave at the end of October, they received a letter from Nestegaard written while he was in Copenhagen, where he had gone to deal with these issues, telling them he would travel with them through America on his way back to China.[71]

St. Paul's church, Minneapolis

The report of the second annual China Mission Society meeting held at St. Paul's congregation in south Minneapolis from June 30 to July 3, 1891, contained the information that a Miss Mathilda Hjermstad had applied to go to China, and she was to be sent with the Rønning siblings. This was published in *Budbæreren* on July 15, 1891, with the report that she would be a teacher and a companion for Thea. Both the Hauge synod and mission society resolved to support her, something they had to be careful about. It was inappropriate to assume that everyone belonged to both the Hauge Synod and the China Mission Society, even though most of them did. Both Thea and Halvor had to write letters saying they belonged to both groups but were most closely knit to the Hauge Synod.[72]

The August 15 edition of *Kinamissionæren* contained the results of a survey of Chinese students as to what they thought China most needed. Most criticisms had to do with the school system, with its rigorous and maybe arcane examinations on Chinese history and literature, which had been under attack for years for not being useful. In addition the situation of women needed immediate reform. Footbinding should be stopped, the students felt, and women should be educated. American readers could agree with those findings, but nothing could be as convincing as the stories which were filling up the journal. One of the most moving accounts appeared in that same issue of the journal. It was from a Miss Butler in Nanjing (undoubtedly the editors were taking many of their stories from English and American mission journals), who reported that a young, very sick girl came into their mission and received help. Although she said little, she went home and then came back a second time. When she left for home again, she said to the missionaries, "I know they will beat me at home, but then I will think of you and pray to Jesus so it won't hurt so much, for I know that you are also praying for me."[73] Such stories only increased the resolve of women like Thea and others in America to do all they could to help less fortunate women in China.

Solør church

That fall Thea and Halvor traveled through southern Minnesota, Iowa, northern Nebraska, and South Dakota, making their farewells to Hauge Synod congregations and raising money for their work. Among the congregations mentioned are those of Pastors Iver Christian Larson Hatlestad (1853-1909) of the congregation in Ossian, Iowa; Gustav Christianson Gjerstad (1856-1919) of the congregation in Clermont, Iowa; Christian Christopherson Holter (1854-1922), of the Nazareth congregation in Iowa; and Lars Harrisville (1864-1925) of Sioux City.[74] As these meetings are described, only Thea and Halvor seem to have been there. Miss Hjermstad by then must have already sensed that she did not really have a call. Even as late as September 13, 1891, at a farewell party in the Rønning home church in Faribault, only Thea and Halvor were present. The excitement, however, was building throughout the Hauge Synod. The history of Rønning's Solør church near Faribault records that "at that time we hardly knew where China was located. A wave of enthusiasm for establishing a mission in China swept the Hauge Synod and not the least Solør church which gave up its beloved minister as the first missionary from the Hauge Synod to China."[75]

A touching report on the evening is printed in the October 15, 1891, *Kinamissionæren,* including selections from the speeches and sermons of Rønning, Oppegaard, Martin Gustav Hanson (1859-1915), and, of course, O. S. Nestegaard the elder, who had just arrived from Europe. Halvor spoke for Thea, saying she was simply too moved to speak. These scenes would be repeated wherever they went, with songs, speeches, offerings for the mission in China, with Thea unable to speak for tears.

In each of these congregations, the Rønnings forged a bond with the people that their letters would maintain. One of the strongest was with the Riverside congregation in Dawson, Minnesota, which had established a Mission Circle in 1885. Thea would strengthen that relationship with many letters, especially to the Junior Mission Band. Its members would in turn write letters to her and send what little they could raise to support her mission activities. Østby reports frequently in the paper that yet another Ladies Aid had begun with the main purpose of supporting the mission in China.

Hannah Rorem

In late September, 1891, the China Mission Society board reported that, although Miss Hjermstad no longer felt the call to the mission and could not leave with the Rønnings, a Miss Hannah Rorem (1871-1907) of the Nazareth congregation near Radcliffe, Iowa, announced she would accompany them. Hannah Rorem had been born November 6, 1871, in LaSalle County, Illinois, where her parents, Torgrim and Anna Rorem, had a farm. She was baptized by Elling Eielsen (1804-1883), the crusty and uncompromising Haugean, the first Norwegian to be ordained in America. When she was a year old, the family moved to Hamilton County, Iowa, and the township of Radcliffe, not far from Ames, Iowa. Her parents were, by her testimony, pious Christians who taught her the faith. Her confirmation pastor, Christian Christopherson Holter (1854-1922), another leader in the Hauge Synod, would go on to become the vice president and secretary of the synod, now and then editing the church paper. In the autobiography Hannah wrote for *Kinamissionæren,* she said she would never forget his word to her when she was confirmed: "Seek ye first the kingdom of God and his righteousness, and all these things will be added unto you."[76] She had attended normal school in Dexter, Iowa, where she trained to be a teacher in a common school. By her own admission in her testimony, she began to stray and follow the broad way in worldly amusements. This is the conventional testimony of a conversion in this tradition. Only after she had taught in a common school for three terms and realized the great responsibility she had for the children did she begin to think of her own soul. This, she said, became most clear when her father died on January 9, 1890. About that same time, a great awakening was taking place in the Nazareth congregation which God used to bring her to the truth. "After a short, but hard battle, I was completely won for Jesus."[77] Very soon after that she began to feel an "inner" call to go forth to the heathen to tell them about Jesus, the Savior of all people. It came when, during a geography lesson in her school room, she wrote down the name "China" and felt irresistably called to be a missionary to China. She did fit the job description for a teacher, though she was a mere nineteen when she accepted the call to China. Her call, however, was not from the China Mission Society, which determined it could not support her. Instead she convinced her six siblings and the local congregation to support her, which they did. The Nazareth congregation, where Miss Rorem was a member, was a strong and flourishing Hauge Synod congregation. She had probably been at the meetings with her family when the Hauge Synod met there in 1886 and discussed a possible mission to China. So her decision, which to others seemed to have been made rather abruptly, was not abrupt for her. The China Mission Society, however, could not meet in time to approve her call and give her official support. Because of this the congregation and her family, aware that they could not expect the society to act that quickly, arranged to support her, especially since she would be able to travel with the Rønnings to China, something they all thought best. The paper carried a description of the meeting where she was commissioned at the end of a series of testimony meetings (*samtalemødet*) held October 21 to 23, 1891, in the Nazareth congregation. Halvor appeared for the last day of the farewell festival and preached a sermon which moved in peoples' hearts like an earthquake (*opploiet jord*). After several more speeches, the pastors knelt at the altar with the young missionaries as the congregation rose and prayed to God "who dwells in the heavenly courts." After that they received an offering of $368.76, more than a single woman missionary recieved in a year! At the closing of the service, Hannah, not only a very beautiful woman, but also a gifted musician, sang a solo, "*O Venner, som forsamlet er.*" ("O Friends Who Gathered Are"). With that the choir sang a common farewell hymn, "*Men skilles vi maa*" ("But We Must Part").[78]

The Rønnings had visited the Iowa congregations before in their travels to garner support. Hannah had most surely heard them speak of their hopes and dreams for the mission in China and been moved. Clearly the Spirit's fire affected the young Hannah. Why she felt the call to go so quickly and with them is never fully discussed in the sources. It is not difficult to think that she had fallen in love with the handsome Halvor and wanted to follow him at any cost. Her Christian missionary conviction, however, was indisputable. One can tell from her letters home and her leadership of the *Missionsdueforening* (Mission Dove Society), a group of missionary wives and single women, that she was more than capable. A story in *Kinamissionæren* published just as the young women were boarding the ship for China seemed almost to speak directly to the Rorem family: Hudson Taylor in *China's Millions* had told of a young woman who, after a mission meeting, felt called to be a missionary, and went up to the altar to give her life to Christ's mission in China. Her father, weeping, had said, "She has been the light of my life—she can't go—but nothing is too good for Jesus." She went with his blessing, and while she was learning Chinese, her young Chinese teacher became a Christian.[79] This was very like Hannah's story, except that her father had recently died.

The Norwegian Roots of Thea Rønning

Torbjørg (Thea)

Thea's parents, Nils and Kjersti Buskerønning

Home of the Rønnings in Bø

Church in Bø where Thea was confirmed

THE JOURNEY TO CHINA

At this time the newspapers and the journal reported increased violence in China along the Yangzi River in what were called Anti-Foreign Riots that were especially vicious. The massacre of two British subjects and riots in Wuxue were described by the *New York Tribune* on August 16, 1891, as being more than an isolated event, but part of a growing rebellion rather like the Taiping Rebellion. But this time it was led by the man the West called the "Chinese Bismark," Li Hongzhang. Although the emperor had decreed that foreigners should be kept safe and the officials should prosecute those who had acted violently against the missionaries, the paper did not think they were eager to do so in the area where the young people were going to begin their mission. It took unusual bravery for the young woman from an Iowa farm to decide to go out on her own. The September meeting of the board of the China mission had seriously considered whether or not to send any missionaries at all to China in light of the disorder there, but decided, after much discussion, to go forward. It then accepted Miss Hjermstad's resignation as its missionary and decided to receive with pleasure Miss Rorem's offer to go at her own expense. The board was overwhelmed that the Lord had filled Miss Hjermstad's empty place and marveled at the resolve of the congregation to support Hannah in a way almost unknown before. "How many congregations in America could easily do the same if only the Lord

"Chinese Bismark," Li Hongzhang

would open people's hearts?"[80] With that the members of the board wished both Hannah and the congregation God's blessings.

On October 13, 1891, Thea wrote her sister at home in Norway a letter of farewell on their leaving for China. "God alone knows what will come of our trip to China, whether we shall meet sorrow and death, or joy."[81] Her hope was that she would be able to use the talent God had given her to bring salvation to the Chinese. "Farewell," she said. "If we don't meet on earth, we will certainly meet in heaven."[82] It was a serious letter that shows she sensed that China was much farther away in time and culture than the United States was from Norway, which she soon would learn was true. A side bar in the letter contains the slogan, "All for God, Jesus for China. Come over and help us!"[83]

There are many descriptions, but unfortunately no pictures of the final leave taking from Faribault on October 28, 1891. All of them tell of the large crowd at the station and the speeches from the train. Østby wrote later in more detail about the impression the Rønnings and Hannah had made on the entire town. The day before their departure, Halvor walked about, saying his final farewells to bankers, merchants, workers, Americans, Germans, and Scandinavians. On Tuesday, October 27, 1891, after a devotional meeting with Halvor, Thea, and Hannah, the entire congregation was invited to a party in the church basement at midnight, a complete surprise to the young people. The next day people gathered around Rønning's house as he tried to pack his suitcases. He had been up the entire night meeting with his people, building them up and hearing their concerns, even leading a struggling young man through a spiritual crisis at the same time. When they got to the depot there was a great crowd. The farewells were stirring. The oldest man in the congregation took their hands and blessed them in the name of the Triune God. Thea spoke of the dry bones in Ezekiel 37, making particular reference to the twenty-third verse:

> They shall not defile themselves any more with their idols and their detestable things, or with any of their transgressions; but I will save them from all the backslidings in which they have sinned and will cleanse them; and they shall be my people and I will be their God.

The emphasis of the missionaries, and especially Thea, was that the Christian God was a living God, not a dead idol.

In her diary of the journey to China, of which only a few pages have survived, Thea, who until now had signed her name Torbjørg, wrote that when they left Faribault the weather was lovely, the sun shedding its friendly rays upon the earth; the day, however, was serious. When the time came for them to bid their last farewells "and travel out to the cold, dark, heathen land of China with the glad tidings of the Gospel," they gathered up their trunks and left the house which was filled with people who gave them over to God's protection. Thea, Halvor, and Hannah left, accompanied by Nils and Pastor Østby to Mankato.[84] Hannah was to say the last words of farewell. It was almost impossible to say anything, she said, for the tears they were all shedding. When they got on the train and it started to move, they could see the hats and handkerchiefs of the people waving goodbye until they disappeared on the horizon. Thea's only comfort was the promise of heaven where "we would meet and never again be parted."[85] As the train moved toward Mankato, she dreaded the fact that here they would have to bid their last farewell to Nils, the Rønnings' brother. Everyone said this was the most difficult farewell for the Rønnings. They changed trains there, Nils and Østby back to Red Wing, and Halvor, Hannah and Thea to Omaha and finally San Francisco. The train to Red Wing came first and, after a quick but tearful farewell, Nils and his siblings were parted. It would be the last time Nils would see Thea alive. As they were waiting for the train, Halvor felt the hand of O. S. Nestegaard the elder on his shoulder. Where he had been since the meeting in August is not clear, but he very likely would have been traveling about, speaking of the mission. He would accompany the three to San Francisco and China. Halvor hoped that he would be a comfort and help since he had traveled that way before.[86] "We were now four. We went to the sleeping car and commended ourselves to God and slept while the fast train carried us hundreds of miles away from our family and friends."[87]

Halvor, in recalling the farewell party in his journal, said it felt almost like a funeral, except for the fact that they knew they would meet again, if not here on earth, then in heaven. He too had been overwhelmed by the many people and the dinner in the basement of the church. When the party was over, however, in the middle of the night, one of Rønning's confirmands came to him and took his hand, crying out that he was lost. "Pray for me! Pray for me!" In the dark, outside the church, Halvor wrote, "We knelt on the cold ground and prayed that God would receive again his prodigal son. . . . I have had several such Nicodemus night meetings in Faribault," Halvor concluded.⁸⁸ These reports indicate how much the people loved him and what a fine pastor he was.

Even as the train forged west, though the hour was late and they were extremely weary, Halvor could not sleep because of a splitting headache. He had a rough night, sleeping and waking, sleeping and waking. Finally he prayed that somehow his pain would lead him to some blessing. He could barely see or hear for pain, he said. While they were waiting for the Union Pacific train to San Francisco in Council Bluffs, he met a Chinese man with whom he spoke for a bit, learning that his parents were still living in Hankow, the Rønning's destination. From that conversation he found a pharmacy where the pharmacist prescribed him something that cured his headache almost instantly. As he spoke further with the pharmacist, telling him about their trip to China, the pharmacist gave him medicines that he could use in China, for which Halvor was most grateful, regarding the headache as God's way of answering his prayer.

Swedish missionaries

While he was at the pharmacy the women strolled through town. Thea noticed a building, maybe a courthouse, with what seems to have been a picture of justice painted on it, with the blind woman holding a scale in her hands. Although Thea appeared not to recognize that it was the traditional figure of justice, it struck her as a sign of what the last judgment would be like. She prayed that she would not be found wanting on that day.⁸⁹ In Omaha, five Swedish missionaries sent by Franson's organization boarded the train on their way to Japan. They shared conversation and devotional times with them. One of the Swedes had a guitar, so they enjoyed singing spiritual songs from the Swedish tradition which the Norwegians knew well. After a good night of sleep, they awoke to find two more missionaries had boarded the train, also on their way to China. By now they had come far enough to see the Rocky Mountains which reminded Thea of her childhood home and the area where she had grown up in Telemark. Miss Hannah, as Thea referred to her, had never seen mountains before and kept exclaiming on how beautiful they were. Now deep into the mountains they saw hardly any towns or cities, only wild land. Nestegaard, she reported, had found a Jewish man who had never read the Bible and did not know the truth, as she put it. "Yes, there are heathens enough right in the middle of this Christian land," she exclaimed. The next evening in the gathering dusk they met yet another missionary on her way to China, this time an English lady. After a long talk, they went to bed, Thea wrote, feeling safe in the promises of Jesus that not even a sparrow could fall without God's knowledge.[90]

The next day, October 31, as the train made its way through the mountains, they enjoyed singing, praying, reading one chapter of the Bible each, in Swedish, Norwegian, and English. As they were preparing for bed, they heard they would arrive in California the next morning. Most got up early to catch the first glimpses of the state and then the Pacific Ocean. As the train traveled slowly up the coast, they marveled at the dramatic landscape along the ocean, thanking God for bringing them safely thus far. Soon they arrived at their destination and boarded a steamboat that took them several miles to San Francisco where they found a hotel. After a rest and dinner, they went to the Sutro Heights Park in San Francisco. For Thea it was the most beautiful place she had ever seen—lovely flowers with statues along the way, with a view of the ocean where she could watch its long, powerful waves beating against the sandy beach. From there they took a boat back to San Francisco and then went to Chinatown. It was her first taste of things Chinese. Thea wrote in her diary and also in a letter to *Kinamissionæren* how shocking it was to see the idols in the temple, gods who were dead and for the dead, a theme repeated

Hannah Rorem

by many other missionaries in their letters home. Once again she thanked God that he was a *living* God and not dead, a theme she particularly stressed.[91] From there they went to have dinner with Pastor Ole Grønsberg (1855-1931) of Our Savior's (*Vor Frelsers*) Lutheran Church, the Norwegian Synod congregation in San Francisco. On Monday, November 2, Thea and Hannah stayed in the hotel writing farewell letters to friends and family while Halvor went to buy tickets on the steamship *Oceanic*, the first ship of the White Star Line, now being leased by the Occidental and Oriental Steamship Company to carry passengers from San Francisco to Yokohama and then Hong Kong. It had been plying its way across the Pacific for many years and came highly recommended to him by a missionary on the train, partly because of the design of the ship. It carried 169 first class passengers who could all be seated in one dining room amid ship, away from the vibrations of the motors. Steerage could hold 1000 people divided between single men in the bow with women and families in the stern. When Halvor found out the price of a first class ticket to Shanghai was $300, he tried to get second class, but the agent strongly advised him to go first class, given the ladies who were with him, which turned out to have been good advice. It is nearly certain they could not have tolerated conditions below deck. Halvor bargained with the agent for a good deal, saying that they were the first missionaries to go from their group, and if they liked it many more, on their recommendation, would sail with them. He got the tickets for $163 apiece, plus $80 off all four, and he remarked to himself, "Well done!"[92]

Before they sailed the next day on November 3, 1891, Thea took out her Bible, read it, and prayed that she would be faithful unto death.[93] After packing and getting things ready, they went to the Swedish church where they had a farewell service and dinner, and then were followed to the ship by a number of the congregation. At 3:00, the ship steamed out of the port to the singing and *adieus* of the people on the pier. When they got out some distance, fog closed in on them and the ship dropped anchor where they stayed through the evening. Through the fog, however, they could see the lights of San Francisco. Halvor marveled at the sight and thought of the day when he would sail into the heavenly harbor and see the lights of the New Jerusalem. Thea was awed by the San Francisco night as well, but what had impressed her most were their decidedly upper class accommodations and food, the likes of which this young farm girl from Norway and Minnesota had never seen before.[94]

On their third day out, November 4, at noon, they sailed into a storm which made many on board sick, especially Thea. Halvor went down into steerage to see the Chinese there, packed like sardines into a tin, he said. It was for him a moment of truth: The smell of the Chinese, the way they ate, and their bad hygiene shocked him.

> These are the people I will be living and working with for the rest of my days. Uff, fy! No, no, be still, my proud heart. Think of Jesus, God's only Son who went deep, so deep, that no one can know. If I can only save some of the poor stinking heathen out of their heathen ways, out of eternal death, what should I not be willing to suffer? Yes, I am willing, Lord Jesus, to give all of my working days, my whole life and set it on the altar of missions. You must give me the ability, for our abilities come from God![95]

Thea remained seasick and spent the next few days in bed. Hannah, she reported, was not sick. From the diary, we can infer that Hannah, the more educated and experienced in life, was the more hardy and capable, leading Bible studies and prayer meetings. Halvor wrote that while Thea was very ill, Nestegaard, not surprisingly for a madman, was not affected by seasickness. He was able to help the sick Japanese and Chinese below deck where he spent his time during the journey. Hannah, Halvor noted, was *"frisk som en fisk,"* a Norwegian rhyming phrase that means "healthy as a fish." He started calling her by her first name now and noticing her commendable qualities. Thea, as she began to recover from her nausea, gathered strength from remembering those who were praying for them both in Faribault and home in Norway. During the storm a Chinese man in steerage died and was buried at sea. This struck Thea hard because she knew he was not a Christian and believed he would be there until the sea gave up its dead, and not found among the saved. [96]

As they got their sea legs they were able to enjoy the voyage more and more, getting to know their fellow passengers. Halvor spoke with a rich Chinese man who respected Christianity but had not converted. Later he met a wealthy Japanese man who had traveled the world, and while he was impressed with some of Christianity, he was appalled by the ungodliness of many so-called Christians. As Halvor spoke with him he realized how much one needed to know to represent Christianity effectively to someone like this man. A missionary to Japan, Halvor concluded, had to be educated and smart. This did not auger well for the Swedish missionaries, he thought, casting aspersions on Franson's society for sending uneducated people to such places like Japan or China.[97]

On November 6, Hannah celebrated her twentieth birthday, which they marked by giving her some small gifts and blessings. For devotions they read the story of Jonah and thought of their own calling in relation to Jonah's refusal to go to Nineveh. They prayed as they did frequently to be able to give their wills over to God so that they would do what he wanted and also what would be best for them. It is perhaps hard for us to understand this prayer today. The changing of one's will, for these young Haugeans, was a serious struggle of the soul. To give over one's will to God was a matter of prayer and tears, and the records of their spiritual struggles focus on this more than any other theme.

The journey continued through storm and good weather. We have a few bits of Thea's thoughts during this time, but we also hear about her from Halvor's diary. On November 11, Hannah came into him shrieking with horror. A Chinese man had died on the lower decks and the Chinese were trying to send away the evil spirits that accompanied his death. Since it was not the custom in China that the dying should die in their beds, they had taken him on to the deck where they burned his flesh in order to chase out the evil spirits. It was more than either he or Hannah could bear to watch, but it did make them think deeply about the world into which they were traveling. The only comfort he could find was from Mark 10:27-30, that all things were possible for God, "Truly I say to you there is no one who has left mother, wife, children and fields for the sake of my gospel who shall not receive in return hundredfold."

The next day Halvor took his usual walk around the deck and went down to the Chinese to see how they were doing. "With sorrow I see their uncleanliness, I wonder what it would be like if a huge wave came over the deck and washed them all. Yes, they all need a good bath from head to foot."[98] This culture shock, however distressing, did not weaken his resolve to be a missionary. Given the number of missionaries on board, he took the opportunity to dis-

The Journey to China | 73

cuss the Chinese culture and the best mission strategies with them. A medical missionary, Dr. Robert Swallow, from the British Free Methodist Church, who had served in China for nineteen years, advised him that the best way to learn the language was to spend time with the Chinese and not be afraid to speak the language even if one's command of it was not good. He also advised him that wearing Chinese clothes, as Hudson Taylor had recommended and as many missionaries did to show solidarity with the Chinese, was unnecessary since they could not hide that they were Westerners.

The closer the four came to Asia, the more serious their thoughts became. Halvor, who had made friends with several Chinese and missionaries to China, began to struggle in prayer to remember the great task they had before them: He had heard that over thirty-three thousand Chinese died every day without having heard a word about Jesus Christ. The need appeared to them to be more and more pressing as they neared China. Several Chinese died while on board, and it troubled them that they had not been able to bring the gospel to any of them. "Teach me to number my days," Halvor prayed in the words of Psalm 90, "so I may get me a heart of wisdom."[99] He noted, as they neared Japan, that the Chinese tended to be short, although those from the north, where wheat was the staple starch, were taller. They had flat noses, brown eyes, and very small hands and feet. Once again he noted their uncleanliness, saying that the impurity of their souls was mirrored in their faces, especially among the old. "My heart burns to help them," he exclaimed.[100]

On November 23, 1891, they woke up in Yokohama, Japan, which looked to them like many a town on the coast of Norway, with mountains rising from the sea around it. They remarked at all the boats from around the world that were docked there. Several of their traveling companions disembarked to begin their work as missionaries to the Japanese while the Rønnings had to gather up their luggage and transfer to the *Kobe Maru* steamship for Shanghai. When the Rønning party had been preparing to leave for China from San Francisco, Japan had experienced one of the worst earthquakes in human history on October 28, 1891, the Mino-Owari Earthquake, with what scientists today record as an eight on the Richter scale. Its center had been near Yokohama, although the city actually suffered little damage to its buildings, according to a report. The devastation elsewhere had been terrible. When the Rønning party arrived almost a month later, aftershocks were still moving the ground beneath them. While awaiting their departure for Shanghai, they traveled by rickshaw to the home of an English seaman's mission led by a Pastor Austin, whose hospitality warmed their souls. When he told them of the earthquake that had taken over 10,000 lives, they were struck as they heard of the earth literally opening its mouth and swallowing so many, that it had occurred in a region where opposition to the Gospel had been most fierce. As they were hearing this story, an aftershock frightened them. They fell to their knees in prayer. The next morning they toured the city and found it to be a lovely city with many Westerners there. They were surprised to see a good number of Christian mission stations and schools. From this report we do not hear that they saw much destruction. What they saw appeared to have withstood the quake. Still, it was a sobering experience for these young people who had never before experienced earthquakes.

At noon they boarded the *Kobe Maru* and began their journey to Shanghai. That night Thea did not feel well and went to bed. During the night she had a terrible dream that she was being chased by a roaring lion who wanted to eat her. Halvor and Hannah came running to her to help her as she prayed, "Jesus, Jesus, help me, hold back Satan!" They remembered the line from Luther's "A Mighty Fortress is our God:" "One little word will fell him" and took comfort in it. Halvor mused on how Satan had driven them to God, who "had with Jesus lifted us out of sin, Death and the power of the Devil."[101]

The ship then docked in Kobe, Japan, where they met more missionaries and Westerners. They were surprised to meet a teacher, Miss Brown, from Carleton College in Minnesota, who very likely was teaching at the Kobe College for Women, and a pastor, Rev. Barclay Fowell Buxton (1860-1946), with the British Church Missionary Society, a very successful missionary to Japan, whose work supported many missionaries in the area. Suddenly Halvor remembered it was Thanksgiving Day in America, and they gave thanks for God's mercies to them. They then went with Buxton to his school where he preached and led a prayer meeting. It cheered the young people to see how this mission was going in Japan, and they blessed him for his generosity as they boarded their ship, the *Kobe Maru*.

Halvor woke early the next morning and went up to the deck to pray and walk around the ship. During the walk, looking at the lovely landscape of Japan behind him, he was overcome with fear and dark thoughts which he could not overcome. He went for a long conversation with Dr. Swallow who advised him that his most important task as a missionary was to keep his health; in the long view, it was the best thing a missionary could do. A sick missionary was nothing but a drain on everybody and their resources. Again the next night he felt that the devil was attacking him with fury. All he had was the Savior's gospel. He went up to the deck and looked at the heavens, the stars where he often looked for help, and heard the word of God most clearly in the words of Isaiah 60:11: "Your gates shall be open continually; day and night they shall not be shut, that people may bring to you the wealth of the nations, with their kings led in procession."

The next morning he read in *The North China Daily News* about the attacks on Christians, especially in Hunan, where missionaries were being attacked and brutally killed. One can feel especially Halvor coming to realize the seriousness of their mission and the dangers before them. Their only refuge was in God and God's Word. That Sunday, they landed in Nagasaki where they were able to attend an English service. After the service and a tour of the local Catholic church, they learned about the ending of the Catholic mission in Nagasaki with the persecution of the Jesuits and the martyrdom of twenty-six Japanese Christians in the sixteenth and seventeenth centuries. They even had time to visit the church built in memory of the martyrs, which had been consecrated in 1862 by the Catholics. Nagasaki had been the center of Catholic mission at the end of the sixteenth century when Portuguese sailors had brought the faith to the island nation. By some estimates there were over 300,000 Christians in Japan before the shogun had banned the religion and crucified twenty-six Christians in 1597. As Halvor looked at the monument, his only comfort was that the blood of the martyrs was the seed of the church. After an edifying sermon by a Methodist pastor, they returned to the ship. As they left, they could see by the moonlight the mountains where the Jesuits had been martyred. They looked at it, soberly reflecting on what they were about to meet in the next days, and then realized they were now sailing the Yellow Sea and in the morning would be in China. The next day, Monday, November 30, 1891, they spent the day collecting their prayers and thoughts for their arrival. As never before, Halvor wrote, "We beseeched the Lord for blessings and the strength to go forth in Jesus' Name into China and do his bidding."[102] They took strength from the fact that at home there were thousands of eyes that were following them, praying that their work would bring a great harvest. They gave their lives and work over to the Lord and went to bed for the last time on the ocean.

ARRIVAL IN CHINA

The next day, on December 1, 1891, they arrived in China, sailing into the mouth of the Yangzi River where the great harbor city of Shanghai was situated. During the nineteenth century it had become one of the largest cities in the world, settled by many international groups brought to the city by trade and diplomatic work. It was the city where Hudson Taylor's CIM was headquartered and where the missionaries would go to find rest and recover from illnesses. It would be something of a safe harbor during the unrest that culminated in the Boxer Rebellion. This party of young missionaries from the Midwest had never been in such a large city before. One wonders what was running through their minds as the ship lay at anchor until the tide rose. "With searching eyes we stood on the deck and waited and waited—finally we saw a long ways off the coast of China!" They watched as Shanghai harbor with its many ships and boats came into view, and then the houses and people. At 11:00, the last hour of the morning, they arrived. As the boat approached the pier, they saw their Norwegian colleague Sigvald Netland standing there with the theological candidate, Johannes Berg Brandtzeg. Finally they were off the ship and had collected their luggage. "With wonderful feelings we stood face to face and shook each other's hands!" With joy the four went with Netland who had rented a house where they could all stay. Thea wrote that it was almost like coming home to arrive at the house,

Shanghai harbor in 1890

where they met two Norwegian missionaries who had recently come to Shanghai, Ludvig Johnson and Sister Berthine Aarestad, a deaconess.[103] Halvor wrote, "I fell to my knees to praise God." Finally, they were in China. His first night, he wrote, "I lay in a Chinese bed that was as hard as stone. If I slept, any time I moved," he wrote, "all of my joints screamed. Thoughts came and went. I am awake on my first night in China!"[104]

The next morning, on December 2, 1891, they received telegrams reporting continuing rebellion and violence against Christians and Westerners in northern China near where they were thinking of building a station. Catholic priests were having their tongues cut out and Christian children burned alive, among other brutal acts. As they considered what to do next, after much prayer and deliberation, they decided, despite their anxiety and the frightening rumors, to travel inland to Hankow, 700 miles west of Shanghai.

Before leaving Shanghai they did some shopping, registered with the American consul's office, and exchanged their money. Later they visited the headquarters of the China Inland Mission, but did not meet Hudson Taylor, its founder. They would, however, keep in touch with this mission throughout their time in China. Halvor would one day serve as a representative to the CIM work from the Hauge Synod. As they walked through the city, Thea was shocked to see the Chinese people and their living situations: "Yes, it is just as we have been told, out in the streets shoemakers, tailors, barbers and all sorts of traders who sit and ply their trades."[105] Furthermore, she noted during the tour of Shanghai, that one had to hold one's nose. To think, she wrote, "right beside the houses lie stacks of coffins with half rotten corpses in them. All they do is cover them with a little straw. It is enough to make one very discouraged."[106] She continued, "One does not need to be hungry in China; one meets on the street people carrying stoves, and the grills are cooking warm food, running after us to see if we will have some. They have chopsticks and cups, naturally, with them; but only the greatest need would tempt us to eat at such a table." The sanitary conditions disturbed her as they did most Westerners, especially those from Scandinavia whose reputation for cleanliness was well deserved.[107] Her culture shock would deeply affect her.

SAILING UP THE YANGZI TO HANKOW

On Friday, December 4, they boarded a steamboat, *Ta-tung,* to travel up the Yangzi River to Hankow. The trip up the river introduced them for the first time to Chinese "coolies" whom they had to hire to carry their baggage on to the boat. Every mile up river brought them into a more and more alien world. On the same boat were other Norwegians, Miss and Mrs. Hattrem and several others from Oslo—a student, Helgeson, and Erickson, a theological candidate, as seminary graduates were called. They had been sent out by a committee in Oslo (Kristiania). Given their common cultural heritage and language, the Norwegians and the Norwegian-Americans found it easy to share the work in China despite their different sending organizations. Together the small band of nine Norwegians shared their common concerns, prayed, and sang together accompanied by Brandtzeg on the guitar as they traveled inland and the river gorge became narrower. They enjoyed the changing landscape with its higher mountains and plateaus and thought it not only beautiful but rather like the fjords and coastlands of Norway.

That Sunday they hired a room on the ship so they could hold services together as Norwegians. Halvor says they fell to their knees praying for their own work and the Chinese. By early afternoon they docked at Wuxue. It was here that the Chinese rebels had recently killed Westerners, a British custom official Green, and William Argent, a missionary for the British Methodists. The shocking story of the murder of the missionaries filled them with horror. According to those who had seen their remains, the bodies showed over fifty knife wounds, and Halvor reported later that he had been at a service in Hankow where they had laid a memorial stone in their memory in a graveyard. Halvor later spoke of his fear and anxiety thinking of such an attack. The mission station in Wuxue, which had been burned down, was now being rebuilt, but the builders had to labor "with one hand," ready to protect themselves with the other hand.

Norwegian missionaries to China 1891
Back row, left to right: Ludvig Johnson, Johan Skordahl, Ole M. Sama,
Front row, left to right: Britta Westervig, Hendrik Seyffarth, Knud L. Stokke,
Johannes Brandtzeg, Sister Berthine Aarestad

After a brief excursion into the city, the missionaries sang and testified to the Chinese on board who were extremely curious. Halvor reported their curiosity went so far as to make them want to touch his starched shirt and take off his shoes so they could see how they were made. The missionaries would often report on the curiosity of the Chinese and usually found it odd, but not hostile. When one thinks of how rarely Western people had been in these parts, it is probably understandable. These missionaries took it as friendly and supposed that the violence against other missionaries had been led by Buddhist priests and authorities who sensed in this new religion a threat to their powers. The missionaries could only grieve that the gospel had not come to China before, and so they tried to witness to the Chinese, but their facility with the Chinese language was small. Halvor retired to his Bible to read just as they passed a beautiful island in the middle of the river with a Buddhist temple crowning the top of the mountain on the island. This increased their eagerness to learn Chinese and speak of the living God to the people there.

HANKOW

On Thursday, December 8, early in the morning, their boat approached the Hankow harbor, but on account of fog they could not disembark until noon. An English missionary came on board to advise them to stay in Hankow for some time until they got their bearings. He reported, to their great joy, that despite the uprising against Christians and foreign devils, several Chinese had become Christians in the last few days. This was indeed good news for the anxious group of missionaries.

Finally, as the fog burned off, the boat steamed in to the landing at Hankow. As the boat approached, suddenly they began to call out at the same time that they could see Daniel Nelson and Ole S. Nestegaard the younger, waiting for them, boarding their boat to welcome them to China. Nelson had moved to Hankow from Wuchang for reasons of safety. The Rønnings were

Street in 1890s Hankow

to stay with the Nelsons, whose home gave the young missionaries a safe harbor while they began to figure out where they would go. With great thanksgiving the now twelve Lutheran missionaries heard Nelson read Psalm 107, after which they all knelt down and gave thanks and praise for their safe arrival. Then Brandtzeg greeted their hosts from the mission friends in Norway and Rønning from the friends in America as the Norwegian and American flags waved in the breeze. Nelson's daughter Norah had prepared a sign, "Welcome to China," it read, with a quote from Isaiah 52:7: "How beautiful upon the mountains are the feet of those who bring good news."

Later Daniel Nelson would describe the meeting from the point of view of those waiting on shore.

> The dining room, serving also as a reception room, was beautifully decorated in green. A welcome greeting in Norwegian and Chinese with large red letters hung on the wall. We were waiting for guests. Soon we saw smoke from the steamboat coming up the river which was to bring a group of missionaries from America and Norway. Oh, how happy we were! No disappointment this time. The boat draws up to the dock. There we see the tall, young, courageous Rev. H. N. Rønning waving his hat. There is the smiling Miss Thea Rønning and there we see Miss Hannah Rorem waving her handkerchief and there was Netland, who met the party in Shanghai. We also see some we do not know. They are representatives of the China Mission Society from Norway. We had a crowded home that evening, an evening with prayer and praise. The future looked bright and it was so wonderful to be messengers to the heathen.[108]

After a good night of rest the group discussed where they were to stay until they decided upon a place to locate their work. Netland, who was returning to Shanghai, had rented a house for them in Wuchang, across the river, where at first they were reluctant to go, given the unrest in the area. After prayer and more deliberation, they decided to move into the home in Wuchang. They packed up their luggage and got into small boats and crossed the river—Wuchang being one of three cities at the mouth of the Han River where it joins the Yangzi. (Wuchang has now merged with Hankow and Hanyang to form one city, Wuhan.) The home that had been prepared for them was quite large, Thea reported, with many rooms, but not all of them were usable. The windows had not yet been covered, so Thea said that she could lie in her bed and look up at the lovely sky, something that both Halvor and Thea did when they needed to find solace, as they had at home. The sky at least was clean and beautiful, and the stars reminded them of the troops of angels God could send to them.

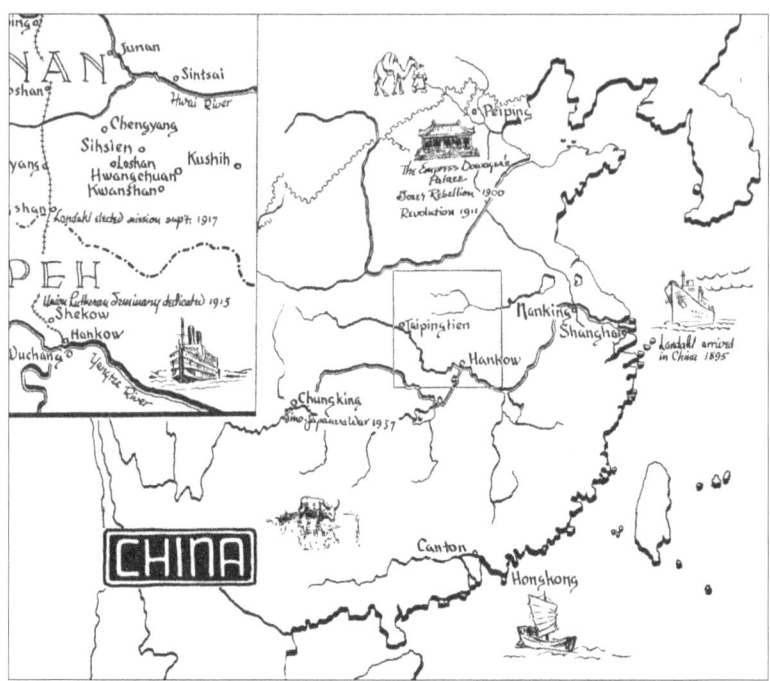

Map of the Hauge Synod mission field in China

Their reports showed them to be aware of the beauties of the Chinese landscape. On their trip across the Yangzi River to Wuchang at the mouth of the Han River, Thea enjoyed seeing that the trees were still green, even in December, that nature was lovely, with mountains, hills, and valleys passing by. The situation on the ground, however, was another matter. "We poor women have now experienced that we are in China; we cannot go out walking in the streets alone without a man. That will be sad until I get used to it." All of the missionaries remarked on the constant noise outside their compounds. Thea noted that it was not the best conditions for sleep, "with canon being shot, drums beating, and every kind of racket through the night." She was not sure they would be very safe in the house, except that there was a "troop of Chinese soldiers barracked behind their house, although some had said they would turn their guns on them at the first opportunity."[109] Her only comfort was that they had a greater and stronger protector in the heavens. The difference between what she was experiencing and what she had known from Norway and Minnesota was hardly describable. Another visitor to China, Count Peter Vay de Vaya, Luskod, a practiced

84 | Thea Rønning

travel writer with more powers of description than Thea or Halvor, wrote about his first encounter in China, about 1902:

> For the first time I saw a real Chinese town in all its immensity. It appeared an inextricable labyrinth of streets and alleys overflowing with people. All our Western ideas are reversed here; indeed, buildings and people alike seemed to belong not only to another hemisphere, but to another planet. The lines are so strange, the colours so brilliant, the sounds so sharp, that one is at once deafened, blinded, and astonished.[110]

The situation in China with its continuing anti-foreign riots which would culminate in the Boxer Rebellion in 1900 had become more and more dangerous. The missionaries reported that every day they expected to hear that war had been declared. The United States had sent war ships to patrol the Yangzi River as far as Hankow in 1891 to protect American businessmen and missionaries that were flocking to the country—not only for the business opportunities, but also because of Hudson Taylor's clarion call to evangelize China by the end of the century. This gave the missionaries some sense that they had some other haven in a time of danger, but they spoke very little of that possibility.

Hankow in 1890s

Still life went on. The Christmas holiday came quickly, and the young people gathered in Wuchang and celebrated a Norwegian Christmas Eve. That day brought more than the regular Christmas excitement and may have surprised the group, although we do not know for sure. Halvor reported that some days before Netland had spoken with him about their living situation and felt it was inappropriate for him to be in the company of the single women, meaning Hannah, so he would have to live in another house rather far away from them in the city. Halvor reported the conversation in a letter to Østen Hanson and said, "I decided to put everything in order immediately and said, 'I will marry Miss Hannah Rorem on Christmas Eve.'"[111] This quickly solved their living problems. Whether they had fallen in love on board the ship or Hannah had fallen for Halvor when he came to the Nazareth congregation and she and he had spoken of marriage is impossible to know from the sources we have. If they had thought of such a thing before leaving for China, it is strange they did not marry before leaving. The report of the wedding from both Halvor and Hannah make it seem more like a marriage of convenience than anything, something not unknown among the missionaries at the time when marriages for romantic reasons were perhaps ideal, but still not the norm. My hunch is that Hannah fell in love with Halvor who did not quite notice it in all the rush of leaving, but that Thea may have taken note of it and may have been slightly put off by what she clearly saw as the designs on her brother by "Miss Hannah Rorem" as she called her somewhat archly in the English phrase in her letters home in Norwegian.

It may account for the letter home to Østby a few days later. In it she speaks very frankly of her despair and feelings of abandonment. She wrote that she could not speak of her Christmas Eve and did not mention the wedding at all. Instead she reported that she had a cold, almost as if to say the wedding did not matter. What did matter was they were living in a house without windows or doors so her health suffered because it did not provide much defense against the winter winds. For Thea, Christmas Eve should have been, she wrote, an evening of joy and a festival, which it was for the others, but not for her. She felt ashamed to say, it and she treats it as a spiritual problem having to do with her own soul. She could have felt guilty for being unprepared for her brother's wedding, but it sounds more like a spiritual struggle of another sort. It is somewhat surprising that the editor printed the letter with its despair.

Halvor and Hannah Rønning

Why she does not mention the marriage of her brother to, by now, her close friend leaves us with questions, but there is not a whisper of ill feelings between Hannah and Thea except for the arch moniker, "Miss Hannah."

What effect this had had on Thea is not clear, but she writes that she had awakened at 5:00 on Christmas Day morning to the sound of a drum and, hastily, had made ready to go to their Swedish counterparts for the Julotta service. Together they sang "Thy Little Ones, Dear Lord, Are We" and then knelt and prayed to the "living" God. Being around the Christmas tree reminded them of the living tree in heaven. At 8:00 they left for home in the sunshine which gave her joy, but she was still troubled. After breakfast they all went to their rooms. Thea writes that she strode back and forth praying that God would bless her so that she could be glad in the Christ child. She received, however, no answer. "I felt abandoned by both God and man." She threw herself into her bed and wept until she heard the call to come to dinner. "I stood up and tried to hide my feelings and went to the table." One can suppose, also, she was now realizing the enormity of the decision she had made to leave Minnesota and come to China. Although she did have the support of her brother and the others, she seemed to feel very alone at this time, the culture shock overwhelming.

After the meal, which she described as very good, she returned to her room where she put on her coat and hat and continued pacing the floor, trying to drive away her thoughts. Finally, she knocked on the door of Netland, not her brother. After some conversation they went out and stood on the city walls and looked at the river and the city. Below them she saw masses of people going about their daily tasks without a notion of Christmas, Sunday, or the living God. Before them stretched a huge graveyard which made her think of Judgment Day, when all these millions would rise from their graves. "There will not be many from here who will meet Jesus in the skies," she concluded.

On their way home, she wrote, the Chinese thronging around them called out, "Foreign devils." She went to her room before the evening devotions of the missionaries and began reading her Bible to find peace. Halvor, having heard of her distress, came in and talked with her. Even after their talk and the devotions, she returned to her room still unable to sleep, although by then she was able to say that the Lord provided. During the morning devotions on St. Stephen's Day, she said, Netland spoke about the martyr's life. It comforted her and then, she said, the storm was over and she was able "to be glad in the Christ child, my Savior, and Redeemer, praise be his name!"[112] Without a doubt, his meditations were prepared with her distress in mind and, as spiritual as she was, the story of a martyr must have been exactly the right topic to discuss that morning.

The next week. after the Western New Year's celebration. they were to begin studying Chinese—something Thea was eager to do. She appeared to have weathered the storm of her despair and enjoyed the visit of some Chinese women. She signed her letter, "Pray for me. Your young and needy servant who craves your intercession." That Østby would publish the letter in all its need and despair is surprising, except that it appears that he had a purpose. Under her signature was a note from Østby remarking on the fact that "Our friends in China, who have given up everything to bring the Gospel to China are living in a house with no doors and windows of paper, where the wind and weather come in freely while we enjoy all the comforts of home, free from hunger and the cold. I wonder, if we cannot all say together: 'Come, let us build them a home?'"[113]

About this time, Hannah wrote a letter, with no date, describing their situation in what sounds like good spirit. She also reported her shock at the conditions in China, finding the need almost overwhelming. She described them sitting and studying their Chinese in their house, now with some windows and doors they could at least close, still feeling the wind blowing through it, only to be interrupted by an unbidden "visitor" entering at any time.[114] Whether this was another person, animal, rodent, or something else is not quite clear, but her account of it was tinged with complications. "I often wonder," she added, "how God feels, when from his throne he looks down on all of these needy creatures. None of them," she concluded, "went to their graves without the tears of God's Son running down over their heads." She concluded with the need they saw and all that had to be done simply to relieve the extreme situation of so many Chinese, especially the children.[115] After language studies, the next most important thing for them was to find a place to build a home and begin their work. Later Hannah would announce the marriage in a letter home almost as an afterthought. "To change the subject, you will maybe be surprised to hear that two of us have exchanged the unmarried estate for the married one, namely Rønning and I myself.... Pray for us, dear brother, that God's blessing will rest upon us so we can continue our journey to heaven and try to win souls for Jesus."[116]

Halvor wrote about their situation in their "unworthy house," with the name Ta-fo-ti. He described it as a stone house not far from the Yangzi River where the Netlands, the Rønnings, and Thea lived. They had a cook, a servant, and two Chinese teachers. They still wore American clothes and ate Chinese food made the American way. He liked the rice, the sweet potatoes, and the meat and fish they could buy in Hankow. Because the city had a concession (a foreign government district) where they could buy most anything from around the world, they did not feel deprived, although they wondered what it might be like when they moved north to begin another outpost for their mission. Each week several large steamboats traveled between Hankow and Shanghai. Given the fortunate location of the city, they thought it was a good place from which to strike out further into the inland. He then announced that they had met with Griffith John (1831-1912), their neighbor in Hankow, who had served in China for thirty seven years with the London Missionary Society. Fluent in both written and spoken Chinese, he was the translator of the Bible into Chinese that the Protestant missionaries preferred and the Hauge Synod missionaries voted to use. An eloquent preacher, he gathered many Chinese around him for his sermons and had a vibrant congregation in Hankow. He built schools, hospitals, and other institutions of mercy along the Yangzi Valley and served as something of the grand old man for any number of young missionaries who arrived in Hankow. John advised the young Norwegian-Americans to keep their headquarters in Hankow, but to build their outpost in the northern part of the province of Hubei. John reportedly knelt with them and prayed for a place where they could found a mission. After his prayer, he stood up and pointed to the city of Fancheng, 300 miles north of Hankow on the Han River. From there they could send workers to Hubei, Henan, and Shaanxi. Fancheng, he said, was a rather large city where two women missionaries from the CIM had moved and begun studying Chinese. The city was a mere four days away by river or land. Halvor and those with him decided they should go there and begin a new field. The advice from John was reported in several letters home, even from Nestegaard the elder, who was under increasing suspicion from the Norwegian mission society and who now had left them for parts unknown, probably Mongolia. The restlessness of the Nestegaard brothers brought them into contact with mission supporters around the world, but it is not difficult to understand that the mission boards were made uneasy by their wanderlust and the unstable character of the elder brother.

Halvor's letter to Griffith John

In the January 1892 issue of *Kinamissionæren*, Østby wrote that, although there had been many reports of the unrest in China and of missionaries being killed, the problem was not really with the missionaries being there, it was that the Chinese were sick of the current regime, were feeling that it was exhausted and that its mandate of heaven had disappeared. Hudson Taylor had written the supporters of his mission that the Christian response to this unrest was to love the Chinese, not shoot them with revolvers.[117] It had been a bad year for China with the droughts and floods, and now the unrest seemed to be increasing. A report in the *Missionary Review* from February 1892 concluded that the worst of all in the Chinese system was that not one in a thousand mandarins had any idea of what to do.[118] Halvor wrote home to say that the unrest roiling about them would lead to some kind of collapse and that the older missionaries they knew felt it would almost be a good thing if the regime collapsed because everything was so bad, nothing worked."[119] The March 1, 1892, issue of *Kinamissionæren* contained a long article on the scourge of opium in China. Because the Chinese associated its spread in China with the British and the missionaries, most of the missionaries agreed it was the worst thing the British Empire had ever done. Hudson Taylor was reported to have written that no Chinese man would convert if he were an addict. They would even sell their children into slavery and their daughters into prostitution. The association of the missionaries and opium was one of the most difficult problems for the missionaries. One can also see that, despite their feeling of cultural superiority and belief in the manifest destiny of the West, they were increasingly quick to oppose insensitive policies driven by what we would see as the racist policies of their home countries. *The Yellowstone Journal* in Montana quoted Taylor, who had recently visited there, on this subject: "After eighty years of contact with England, there are 80,000 Christians, for whom we may be thankful, and 150,000,000 opium smokers for which we may hang our heads in shame. The slave trade, the licensee of immorality, these were bad enough, but the opium curse is the sum of villainy."[120]

SETTLING IN

As the Rønnings began studying Chinese and settling in to their completely new and strange surroundings, they began writing home, not only to family and friends, but also to the two church papers, *Budbæreren* and *Kinamissionæren*. Their letters are vivid accounts, interesting even at this remove. What they related to their audiences are events and encounters that showed the people back home what their circumstances were and how their gifts were both needed and appreciated. Both Hannah and Thea were very aware that their letters were necessary to keep and intensify the interest of their supporters, especially women, who responded with prayers, money, and other gifts. The editors of the papers shrewdly kept publishing such letters both to and from the missionaries. In the March 15, 1892, issue of *Kinamissionæren*, a woman wrote in to say that the letters from the missionaries had moved her to help. Mathilde Haugerud had started a girls' missionary society to help raise interest in the China mission. In the same issue, Lavine Røkke wrote to say how close she felt to the two sisters she had in China.[121] Such letters from the home base appeared in every issue of the paper.

Thea's main response to the new world in which she found herself, however, was one of shock at the extreme need that swarmed around her. It quite overwhelmed her and wearied her, though she did set to learning the language with enthusiasm which impressed Halvor. He reported in a letter on January 5, 1892, that Sister Thea "is going at her Chinese with vigor," despite the difficult living circumstances where it was so cold he had to write the letter with his gloves on.[122] As Thea was writing letters home describing the conditions of China, two more young women, Olava Hodnefield and Oline Hermanson (later Netland), were beginning to hear the call and would arrive in the next year. Thea's health was not altogether strong; she was sick several times that year. Although nothing was spelled out, clearly her spirits were not always high.

On April 11, 1892, Thea wrote a long and detailed letter to *Kinamissionæren* about their situation, clearly aware of the hunger at home for such reports about their life in China. After the typical spiritual greeting and praise to God for grace and her increasing concern that she would learn the language so she would tell the Chinese about Jesus, she assured her readers that her spirits were good and she felt more and more at home. At this writing she could say that she was in the place where God wanted her to be. Apparently she had gotten a letter from Østby, her spiritual mentor, saying that these times of despair were God's way of cleansing her heart and showing her that she must decrease and Christ increase. Still, she did express, as she did frequently, a yearning to be done with it all and go home to be with Jesus. After these assurances, she went on to answer his many questions. There were now five in the house, along with Sister Berthine Aarestad. The others lived about a mile away. Thea was pleased that their food was good; they could get lamb, beef, chicken, fish, potatoes, rice, whole wheat bread, coffee, tea, and milk. Their cooks had learned to cook for an English family, so they could prepare food in a Western manner for the five. Rice was served at every meal, but milk was very expensive and only used on the rice in the morning with sugar. All in all, she concluded, we live about the same as we did at home, except now she had servants and others looking after her needs as she had done for the Spencers and Hansons in Minnesota.

One could hardly describe their living as luxurious, however, because they came from a farm in Norway where the poverty was enough to drive them to America, they were able to do fairly well in such a primitive context. Not only could they easily care for the animals they might prefer for their own food, Halvor could fix things, serving as a handyman and carpenter. He in fact refers to himself as a carpenter in one of his first letters, describing how he has had to put in doors and windows in the Wuchang house where they were living. Some stories of Western mission work assume that many of the early missionaries from the West were essentially establishing colonial outposts along with their Christian work. While one can read the Rønning's disdain for the current Chinese regime, especially its failing leadership and the state of the culture in their letters, these earnest people from the Hauge Synod were not establishing a Lutheran parsonage culture in China. Given the state church from which the

Norwegian-American pastors emerged, they understood parsonages to be cultural outposts as well as churchly centers. From what Thea, Halvor, and Hannah write, they do not have that sense of bringing a cultural tradition with them in quite the same way. The Rønning siblings had gladly escaped the Norwegian class system when they came to America. Thea had remarked on the difference between the parsonage in Norway and the one she experienced in America with the Hansons. They believed the gospel was universal, and it was their call to preach it to all. They had sacrificed everything to come to China because they wanted to save souls. To be sure they thought that making Christians out of these people would make them kinder, cleaner, and better off, but one has to say in the face of the decay of the empire and the chaos of China at the time, this would not have been difficult to do. China was collapsing. Over the years, as the convenience of having servants and other helpers around them improved their circumstances and made life better for them than it might have been in Norway, they may have developed a taste for such a life, but it was not what they came to do.

They were aware of the cultural differences and cultural superiority of the West for obvious reasons. As we have seen, the first thing they noticed were the unsanitary conditions around them, a dangerous stew of germs that caused diseases such as cholera, typhus, and other communicable diseases that rage when raw sewage runs freely in the streets. Illnesses that were somewhat endemic in China struck the missionaries especially hard. They had been warned by the older missionaries to take good care of their health because, as Halvor had reported earlier, a sick missionary was a drain on everyone. Thea repeated that advice as she was describing their lives, including the diet of the Chinese with whom they did not eat—more vegetables on rice, especially cabbage and garlic, a rather strange vegetable to Norwegians. She then told how they cooked the meal, how the stove they had brought with them from Shanghai could give warmth to the room; but the Chinese used them only to warm their feet, of which she disapproved since it meant the house was always cold.

In their home they had two teachers helping them learn the language for six hours a day. Their teachers, neither of whom were Christians, received five dollars a month. Thea assured her readers that they had still not decided about whether or not to wear Chinese clothes. While both men and women wore similar outer jackets, it was the bound feet of the women she exclaimed over. Essentially made handicapped by this practice, the women could only hobble on their feet, really only stumps. She rarely saw the women, she said, because their handicap kept them inside. Thea and the other women with her did not go out much since the children would flock around them and beg, nearly overwhelming them and making them feel physically as well as emotionally threatened. It was too much for her.

Because Rønning, Brandtzeg, and Nelson had gone to Fancheng where Griffith John had recommended they begin their work, the women were left in Hankow. Before the small group made the decision to build a station there, they wanted to get a sense for the place: how easy access would be to European goods and how difficult life might be so far inland. Still trying to understand how best to preach the gospel and live it, Thea wondered again, as she wrote in a letter to Østby, whether or not they should wear Chinese clothes. The only issue was what would further their mission. She would happily do so for the sake of Christ, who would give them the wisdom to decide, she concluded, for Christ had brought them here to plant and water. *Christ* would give the growth. With that she bid Østby farewell with requests for prayer and the hope that one day they would be gathered together in heaven. Her answers make clear that Østby had clearly been concerned about her and her state of mind. In them there is evidence of her growing sense that she can survive, even flourish, when she gets adjusted. It sounds something like her first evaluation of living in Minnesota with Halvor and Nils. She was probably the kind who first saw the difficulties and then the possibilities. One can gather from her letters that she adjusted slowly to new situations, even if she had the courage to go forward despite all the dangers. For one with this type of a personality, routine and familiarity breed success. From her letter we can see that their lives had settled into a routine of six hours a day of Chinese lessons with their teachers and then their normal chores.

About a month later, in May, Hannah wrote home describing their life together. They had taken in a young boy of about nine, Sun Wang, whom she was teaching English an hour a day after their hours of Chinese lessons. Hoping to plant the good seed of the faith in his heart, she was hopeful it would thrive, given that his parents seemed friendly to the faith. The strategy of the missionaries frequently involved teaching someone like Sun Wang English and the faith, and then watching as he would tell his friends about Jesus. Like the Samaritan woman, they hoped he would call them to come and see. Hannah rejoiced to hear from him that he was telling his little friends about Jesus. He had a huge mission field, they could see, in the small boys running half-naked in the streets, dirty and without any seeming concern from their parents. This shocked her and made her pray that they could help the Chinese convert, because she believed that, with a Christian sensibility, the families would be much more kind and concerned for each other's welfare. Hannah's report illustrates clearly what all the mission boards had come to understand: Women missionaries would have easier access to the families, the women and children with whom they worked daily in the home. It was for the women that both Hannah and Thea had felt the call, and the dire situation of women in China moved many women in the West to support the missionaries in China. Even fairly conservative mission board leaders such as Lars Dahle had somewhat reluctantly come to the decision to recruit women. Nestegaard was very clear on this in his work as well. From his work with the China Inland Mission and Taylor's lieutenants, he had come to understand that the women of China could be most successfully evangelized by other women. Hannah's report on the young boy is the first in what became many stories, almost always personalized with a name for people to remember in prayer and to whom they would send gifts.

The *Missionary Review* of March 1893 featured an article favorable to women missionaries, describing their lives as being "forever busy." Among their many tasks were the schools, teaching the Bible women teachers, looking after the women in the new churches, showing mercy to the old, the young, the feeble, the well, and all sorts of people. In addition they had to care for their families and provide for strangers. "The husband is to be a little civilizing, as a sort of secondary work, but the wife has to keep her eye on him to prevent his being barbarized while he is about it."[123] The fear of missionaries going native, even of marrying a native woman, was something the mission societies worried about. This probably was one of the reasons it was even more shocking when Anna Jakobson fell in love with a Chinese man and did not get permission from Hudson Taylor to marry for some time.

By the end of January, the young women were beginning to scout out their surroundings in Wuchang. The previous Sunday they had gone across the river to Hankow for the dedication of a church which Griffith John had established during his thirty years there. What was most remarkable about this event is that the Chinese congregation had, with its own means and labor, built the church. It must have been encouraging for the young missionaries to attend such an event and see the work of a lifetime coming to fruition. To see the face of the old missionary, Griffith John, joyfully looking out over the congregation he had worked a lifetime to build moved them greatly and encouraged especially Hannah. He had lost two wives in China and was now alone. After the service he had once again urged the Norwegians to go to Fancheng and start a new mission station there.

Rønning, Brandtzeg, and Nelson had, in fact, been scouting the possibilities and were not with them at the time of Hannah's letter. It was lonesome without them, she said, but then demurred—one was not lonesome when one had Jesus. She concluded her letter with a brief description of the Chinese devotions they had every morning: They would read some verses from the Gospel of John and then listen to a short, edifying talk on the text by the teacher which concluded with a prayer. "They are very happy times, even if we don't understand everything."[124]

Because the needs of China appeared right before their eyes with increasing urgency, they were impatient to learn the language well enough to give testimony to the Chinese, even at the risk of their health. The missionaries had been warned to take care of their health for good reason. They could see it from their own experience. Johannes Brandtzeg had become very ill, so ill he was not expected to survive. He did, however, and in his letter to Østby from Wuchang in April 1892, he reported on his recovery, with many thanks to his American colleagues for their help. While being ill had helped him grow spiritually, he said, the cost to the others was too much. His report on what the others had to do for him gives a clear picture of that strain such an illness brought to those who were well and preparing to work with the Chinese. Both Halvor and Netland had to sit with him during the night, risking their own health. In addition, Johnson and Sister Berthine made other sacrifices to care for him by temporarily abandoning their language studies. His description gives a clear picture of what happened when one of the missionaries got sick. In a way the fact that they all lived in close quarters helped because they were able to share these burdens, but the sacrifices of the missionaries in this one case give a clear picture of what it cost the others to care for a sick colleague, especially when they were trying to gather up their strength to establish their mission station.[125]

Sister Berthine, soon to marry Sigvald Netland, wrote a letter reporting pretty much of the same as the others, but she gives us a slightly more textured picture of their work and life together. She rejoiced that their men were not simply "ordinary" pastors with no practical skills, but men who could wield both ax and hammer. Because of their skills in carpentry, the house in which they were living was much improved—a good thing now that it was getting warm. The heat of the Chinese summer was still unknown to them, but from what they had heard they sensed that an airy house could be a good thing. She found it comforting that they were living together in close quarters. She found strength in being together with Halvor as the house father and Hannah as the house mother. Netland, who played guitar, was the song leader who led them in singing at the meals. On Sundays they met with their Swedish counterparts, which also gave them encouragement. They could celebrate common church festivals together, as well as their daily rounds of activity. Their holiday celebrations had been occasions for them all to gather together and share in worship and feasts, something she found to be quite precious. Surely, she said, the Lord has prepared a table for us in the presence of our enemies. This is an interesting use of the verse from Psalm 23. It is very clear that these young people felt themselves to be surrounded by forces that were more than just culturally different from them. They were quite clear that there were powers and principalities lined up against them as well.

LIFE TOGETHER

The letters give us detailed pictures of their time together and show how Halvor became the leader among them. When they celebrated Palm Sunday at their house, which they called "Ta-fo-di," Brandtzeg had preached and Halvor had administered the Lord's Supper. Although they did not as yet have a church with an altar, Berthine Netland was glad they did have the Word which Jesus had promised would bring him into their midst. On Holy Thursday they had been with their neighbor Norwegian missionaries in Hankow at the Nelsons; on Good Friday they had traveled over the river to Hankow to be with the Swedes. Later they gathered at the Daniel Nelsons for dinner in the home the Nelsons shared with the Norwegians. Thea and Berthine had stayed with the Nelsons from Thursday until Easter Sunday when they attended the Easter service at Griffith John's church, after which they visited the graveyard where the murdered missionaries from the Wuxue massacre had been laid to rest. The time which they spent with John encouraged them a great deal. As a young woman, Thea saw that his long years in the Word, preaching and living it, had made him a truly holy man, which she could actually see it in his aspect. As she was back home in Wuchang at the end of the Easter holiday, she was eager to begin again the study of the language. It was her calling.[126]

Halvor about the same time told Østby that Nelson, Brandtzeg, and he were going to travel to Fancheng to see about planting a mission center there. They were happy to be accompanied by the Chinese teacher, Mr. Tang, who would help them make their way north as they sold books and tracts; they were glad to see he was an active Christian. The main news of this letter, however, was that the Nestegaard brothers were going to leave them for Tianjiu via Shanghai in order to find Erick Folke before he returned to Scandinavia. Folke, a Swedish pioneer missionary to China, had gone to China on his own in 1887 and established a mission society at first known as Erik Folke's Mission, but soon became the Swedish Mission in China ("*Svenska missionen i Kina*"), which worked closely with the China Inland Mission organization. Folke's work was rather like that of the Nestegaards, awakening interest in the home country for the mission. For good reason they wanted to effect some kind of closer relationship with his mission since they all had a common purpose: the evangelization of China. After that they would go to Shanxi, where Nestegaard the elder would see if it were possible to take up his old mission there. Halvor did not give a hint of any suspicion or disappointment in the Nestegaards. He wished them much grace and wisdom.

Erik Folke

Halvor was hoping that when he returned from the trip to Fancheng they would have received the funds from home to build the mission headquarters in Hankow. Having the funds to build such a building for themselves had become a serious issue. Even though the Rønnings were planning to found a mission further inland, most likely in Fancheng, they needed a place in Hankow as a headquarters where they could have a school, hospital, and orphanage, as well as a home for the missionaries. Daniel Nelson would live there and serve as something of the leader of the Norwegian-American missionaries in China. The legal tangles they had to sort out were daunting, but finally they got the deed to the land and *Kinamissionæren* published it in its entirety in English, either because they knew their readers were hungry for details such as this, or they wanted to have a public record of it.

The missionaries had just lived through their first summer in China and now had a sense for the heat which was beyond their imagining. Norwegians were not used to the extreme heat of the Midwest, which was nothing compared to the heat of China that brought pestilence, especially cholera for obvious reasons, but also heat strokes when their bodies could not keep them cool enough.

As cholera spread in their area, the Chinese who opposed the missionaries had spread the rumor that they were poisoning the water with cholera germs. This had created unrest and made the missionaries targets for violence which, given the huge population milling around, could erupt in a moment anywhere.

Many of the missionaries to China had begun a rather strong campaign during the 1890s to insure better living conditions for the missionaries, especially the women, noting the terrible waste involved in sending young women to China, training them in the difficult language, only to lose them to ill health because of overwork, a poor diet, and inadequate housing. After 1900, the missionaries built a retreat in the mountains in Kuling, along with many other missionaries from around the world, and spent their Augusts there without fail. Griffith John reported that before the missionaries had discovered the mountains as a place of refuge from the extreme heat (which Halvor reported went as high as 125 degrees outside in the sun and 100 in their rooms), the death rate among missionaries was altogether too high. Someone asked John once where the missionaries had gone before Kuling and he had replied, "To the cemetery." For this reason decent living quarters were crucial. Halvor wrote to the Society Mission Friends on September 21, 1892, describing the plans for the new house now that they had finally gotten the money from the China Mission Society and were going forward. They had realized that it would have to be a two-story building of stone, despite the cost. In their planning and getting advice from the Chinese, they had been somewhat surprised to find that a stone house had to have a foundation dug deeply into the earth, which in this area was the extremely fertile but unstable loess, so it could

Griffith John

Life Together | 101

stand on solid ground. This meant they had to dig some five to six feet into the ground. The most important thing for the house was that it have broad verandas to keep out the blazing summer sun so that missionaries would be protected to some extent from the heat. In back of that building would be a smaller building that would hold the kitchen, a place for the servants and teachers, as well as a room for larger groups to gather. The building, Halvor wrote, would be fifty-eight feet by sixty-eight feet. It would cost about $4,000, and they would use a contractor that Griffith John had worked with and trusted. Halvor thought that they would be able to pay the bill by February and was most grateful to the mission at home for the ingathering of funds, which to their joy and thanksgiving was enough to pay for the mission headquarters. These young men dreamed big dreams. At the same time that they were building the station in Hankow, Nelson and Netland had gone to Fancheng to find a property to rent, buy, or even a lot to build a new station where the new arrivals could live and work. As soon as Nelson and Netland returned, the Rønnings would begin preparing to move there.[127]

While Nelson and Netland were scouting out the new mission field, Halvor turned into a carpenter, working with the Chinese to make sure of the carpenters' progress. The Rønnings had moved across the river from Wuchang to Hankow so they could be nearby as they worked on the new building. At the end of November Halvor reported that soon the roof would be finished. Over 100 Chinese were now working with them, and the progress seemed good. In the middle of this work, they heard that Netland and Nelson had found a potential site in Fancheng where they could build their mission compound. Many Chinese were turning to the Christian faith, they reported, and the people seemed friendly to the idea of a mission station there. The Rønnings began to look forward to their new venture where they could begin their own work.

Thea had been ill during the heat of the summer and hoped that the house would be a great boon to them, especially to the women. It was her considered opinion that most American women were not strong enough to live in the poorly built Chinese homes without windows and doors, especially given the severe climate changes, from extreme heat to cold, normal in that part of China. Women who were not strong, she advised, should not come to China, as Hudson Taylor had advised from the beginning. Not even

Missionary house in Hankow

one's desire to tell the Chinese women about Jesus would be enough if one's health and spirit were not up to the challenges of the climate and completely different culture.

Thea's urgency to learn Chinese so she could begin telling the Chinese about Jesus in their language exhausted her, and she felt the stress clearly. While the language was not impossible, she noted, it took long hours of study and time. Despite her minimal education, she had probably understood something about learning a foreign language when she had had to study English on coming to America in order to work in the homes of "the English" as she called the Yankees in America, Thea was not very well educated, which one can see in her private letters home where she writes without much sense for a sentence or paragraph. While they are interesting and show a lively intelligence and a spiritual sense rare even among these deeply spiritual people, they do not show her to be skilled in self-expression. Her letters seem to be filled with the typical phrases of the day, especially the pious talk.

As she gets more deeply into the work, while she was not as despairing as she had been on first arriving in China as her letter to Østby showed, she was clearly daunted by the struggle simply to survive in this hostile climate and culture. One has to wonder, on occasion, why she felt that she had the strength to go to China. Her brother's presence appears to have given her more strength than she might have had on her own. It is doubtful she would have had the initiative to go on her own so far from home without him.

Thea's advice to women thinking of coming to China is a kind of mirror into Thea's soul, showing what she had come to think was necessary for a woman to have in order to come to China. She may have seen that the fervor of many of the missionaries was not enough. Being caught up by the excitement and drama of China did not prevent one from getting sick and dying. Those well-meaning souls who flooded China after Hudson Taylor's call in 1886 for 100 new missionaries in the next year may have been so wildly successful that it brought more missionaries to China than the mission could handle. Sheer enthusiasm and faith was not quite enough without a strong constitution. Death visited many Western missionary families in China and was no stranger to the Norwegian-American China mission: Norah Nelson, Daniel Nelson's daughter; the two Himle children; and Mrs. Netland, all died within their first three years in China. Thea, Mrs. Himle, Miss Fugleskel, and several others would be dead before the turn of the century. Although the missionaries, in comparison to the Chinese, were fabulously wealthy and healthy, they were not immune to the diseases which stalked them on their arrival.

Thea reported that 1892 had been a sad year for China with the floods and famine ravaging the countryside. Once again she grieved over the dire conditions for the Chinese women who had to go about as cripples because of their bound feet. That summer, after the rainy season, the heat grew so intense that Thea became ill. Halvor wrote that they finally gave her up for dead. Kneeling around her bed, they prayed for the heat to break. They had planned to take her to the mountains about 100 miles from Hankow, but her condition grew so serious they could only pray for God to intervene. Halvor reported that the heat did break almost as they prayed, and during the night Thea got much better, sleeping soundly and even finding it necessary to use a good thick blanket over her. She was, Halvor reported, a new person the very next day. Every summer in China from then on, however, she could count on suffering from the heat. She dreaded it.

The publication, *Kinamissionæren*, in order to raise interest and support for the missionaries, especially women missionaries in China, scoured the English and American press for stories that would give their readers a clear picture of what conditions were like for women in China. The January 15, 1893, issue printed a report on the prevalence of infanticide in China by Adele M. Fielde (1839-

1916), a Baptist missionary. A strong feminist, her book on China, *Pagoda Shadows*—especially the chapter "The Extent of a Great Crime"—gave a detailed and horrifying picture of the treatment of girl babies in China.[128] Although the report contained nothing new to the missionaries or the readers of the magazine, this article gave a condensed version of this chapter, with statistics and anecdotes that made the practice extremely vivid and difficult to ignore. In interviews she had conducted with forty women, they reckoned they had, between them, killed forty-eight daughters as infants. From these women had come 183 sons and 175 daughters. Exactly 126 of the sons grew to be ten years old, but only 53 daughters. She figured that sixty percent of the sons had lived to be ten, while only thirty-eight percent of the daughters had. She counted 158 girls who had been killed. The book by Fielde was used to great effect by mission societies in their efforts to get support for their mission work. Fielde, who was raised a Unitarian, had reluctantly converted to the Baptist faith when she agreed to be married to a missionary to China. When she arrived in Siam to marry her fiancé, she found that he had died while she was en route. Despite this, she remained in China for some time working as a missionary because even she had concluded that the cause of this war on girls was both poverty and superstition. With the acceptance of the Christian faith, the parents could rely on God, not their sons, for support; and though Christianity "does not obviate the poverty . . . it presents life in a new aspect; as an opportunity for acquiring moral and spiritual perfection; and for the saddest life often furnishes the best opportunity."[129] This book was and would be the source for many such articles in mission magazines.

Women spinning yarn

Thea's reports home are set in the context of such books by Fielde as she wrote to a girls' society in Minnesota, trying to give them a clear picture of what her work was like in Hankow.

> You would be amazed. The streets are narrow and crowded, we must walk single file. Many are blind, crippled,

etc., and the air is so bad it cannot be described. On the way home from prayer meeting, we had to pass through a crowd at a theater. People began to scream "foreign devils, foreign devils" but we thought of Jesus. The poor heathen! Pray that a wind of Pentecost will convert them. . . . It is a work of patience to sit all day and learn Chinese—we live in a Chinese house with high walls around us. We still don't see much more than the sky of China and we do not know what it is like to live as Chinese. We still wear our European clothes. We have been invited to visit a couple of Chinese families here. It is strange to see women with bound feet limping back and forth on the earth floor. They gave us hot tea but the house was very dirty for it is common to have farm animals live in the house."[130]

NEW FRIENDS ARRIVE

As the year turned and the celebrations of Christmas 1892 were over, the young missionaries began preparing for the arrival of two new women missionaries. Thea summed up what had happened to them over that past year. For her the language was still the greatest barrier, a cause of anxiety for her, given her urgency to tell the Chinese women about Jesus. "Pray for me so I can begin to speak the language well enough so that I can talk to these poor women. There is so much need."[131] She then adds the comment that shows her growing accommodation to China, "When we first came we thought we would die of the smells; now it seems natural. It is hard to win the women because they are not out in public, so we have to begin with the children."[132] That Thea was being changed can be seen from comments such as this. Even if her Chinese was not as good as she would have liked, she clearly was growing more capable in her Chinese and her experience of China.

On January 25, 1893, Olava Hodnefield and Oline Hermanson arrived in Hankow. Thea and Hannah were delighted to have more female companions. The two newcomers kept journals, as Thea and Halvor had of their journey from San Francisco to China. Their experiences and thoughts were remarkably similar. Olava, who had been orphaned before she was a teenager, moved to be with her uncle who lived in Hamilton County, near the Nazareth congregation, the same congregation where Hannah had been confirmed and from which she left for China. She very likely knew her, and very likely had been at the service sending

Olava Hodnefield and Oline Hermanson on their way to China, 1892.

Hannah and the Rønnings to China the fall of 1891. At least it was the same cast of characters. Pastor Eistensen had confirmed Olava and had been Hannah's pastor. Like Hannah, Olava had received a good education in preparation to be a teacher. Hannah's call must have been an encouragement to her.

Although upon arriving in China Olava had been quite ill with an unknown condition, she would have a long and distinguished career in China. She seemed to have a more robust constitution than Thea, with whom she would work closely when they took up their duties together in China. Olava recorded in her journal very similar reactions to Thea's first encounters with the Chinese. The journey across the Pacific and then from Japan to Shanghai and Hankow had traced the same route as the Rønnings, except she and Oline had escaped serious injury when their train collided with another and they were delayed a bit. Going to the Chinese temples in San Francisco disturbed both Olava and Oline, as did their first sight of a Chinese girl traveling back to China to be married, her feet already bound. Perhaps nothing awakened concern in American women about conditions in China with as much urgency as the binding of women's feet. Fielde had also written a vivid chapter, with pictures on this practice, which appear to have been reprinted from book to magazine to yet another magazine. Along with infanticide, this practice also created urgency in the women's groups at home, even as the Chinese themselves were beginning to try to ban foot binding as well as infanticide.

When Hodnefield and Hermanson arrived in Hankow, they were delighted to see that Rønning, Thea, the Netlands, and Daniel Nelson had all come to the pier to welcome them. Hannah was missing from the group; little had been heard from her over the winter. Olava in a letter written on January 26, 1893, to *Kinamissionæren* announcing their arrival in Hankow, explained why Hannah was not with the others at the pier: She had just given birth to a boy, Nilius, on January 22.[133] Oline, who had taken some courses at the Deaconess Hospital in Minneapolis, also was thankful for their safe arrival, amazed that they were now so far from family and friends. The house was still not quite ready for them, so they had to endure the cold and drafty home for a brief time. Their main goal, as it was with all the missionaries upon arriving in China, was to begin studying Chinese so that they could tell the people thronging around them about Jesus.[134] They set about this with an earnestness made more urgent by the need they saw around them, which to them was absolutely unbelievable. "It is difficult to see all this need and not be able to do anything," Oline wrote home immediately upon arriving.[135]

The purchase of two lots in Fancheng by Nelson and Netland where they could build their station excited Halvor especially because now they could start their own mission in a new field. It was the first time, he thought, that missionaries in China had been able to begin a mission field and buy a lot so quickly. Halvor thanked the China Mission Society members for their dependable and generous support. God, he observed, was working in ways he could hardly believe, for which he was grateful.[136]

On February 25, 1893, the Norwegians declared the new mission compound in Hankow was ready to be occupied, especially welcome for Olava and Oline, neither of whom had a room to call their own. Thea reported with pleasure that they were about to have better living quarters, into which they moved on March 15, 1893. They dedicated the station Easter Sunday, April 2, 1893. At the service of celebration each missionary spoke (it is not quite clear if the women spoke), as did two of the Chinese teachers. In addition to the speeches and other festivities, they heard music from a choir, even a Chinese song, as the small group of missionaries, thankful for what God had done for them, was filled with praise.

In the sermon that Halvor preached, we get a good picture of his capacities as preacher and spiritual leader. In it he compared the stone on Jesus' tomb to the difficulties they had experienced on arriving in China, but then to their great amazement and thanksgiving, God had brought them to the celebration of the day. Toward the end of his sermon, he reminded his hearers, and ultimately his readers at home, that in every part of the house he could see evidence of the widow's mite and the rich man's abundance, without which the building could not have been built. This they could never forget. Even in their joy over the building, on this Easter, a heavy stone of sin lay over the Chinese nation and that was why they had built the building and why they had been called to China: to tell the Chinese people the gospel of Jesus Christ.

Riots caused by the anti-foreign pressures were increasing at this time as well as the fury over the Geary Act, which outraged both the

Chinese in America, as well as those inland. The law, proposed by California Senator Thomas Geary, required all Chinese in America to carry identification and "identity" papers, rather like an inland passport, and if they were caught without it, they could be sentenced to a year of hard labor. In addition they had to have "certificates of residence" along with "certificates of identity," a requirement added by the McCreary amendment to the original act. They had to show they had entered the United States legally in order to remain. In order to be legal the certificates of residence had to show the name, age, local residence, occupation, and photograph of the applicant. The amendment denied bail to Chinese in *habeas corpus* proceedings as well as making it the duty of all Chinese laborers in the U.S. to apply within one year for a certificate of residence, with a duplicate kept in the office of the collector of Internal Revenue. It also required that two white American citizens had to vouch for the statement of the Chinese person.

Even though the missionaries were also upset by the act, the Chinese could not make the distinction between America and these Americans or Europeans.

The missionaries in China had set great store by the fact that the nephew of the Empress Dowager was reading the New Testament, and they hoped that he would convert to Christianity and bring the whole nation along with him. Such hopes proved to be futile, but it was clear that the Chinese aristocracy was casting about wildly for some way to curb the dissipation and despair which swirled around them in the streets. Some Chinese looked to the West for help; others blamed the West for all their troubles. Though the missionaries brought medicine and established orphanages and other institutions of mercy, the Chinese resented the missionaries for their associa-

Chinese girls living in the orphanage the missionaries built

tion with the policies of Western imperialism toward China. Most irritating and insulting to the Chinese were the extra-territorial rights which most Chinese did not have in their own country. While the missionaries could understand this, these treaties were the ones they appealed to when trying to get their buildings built.

Thea wrote of being called "foreign devils" by the crowds milling around them, but said she had grown used to it and did not think it meant anything especially ominous. It was just what the Chinese would say on seeing Westerners who were not common in this part of China. The crowds could turn ugly in moments, however, making it dangerous for missionaries to be out in the streets alone. Throughout this decade one can see in the reports of the missionaries the growing reaction against the missionaries which would break out violently in the Boxer Rebellion the summer of 1900.

In April 1893 Oline Hermanson gave a picture of the good fellowship the women were having together in their common work in the Hankow compound, but while she had expected much of their situation to be the way it was, in spiritual matters it was much worse than she could have dreamed. The needs in China, especially among the women, were far more serious than she had expected. Their inability to speak to the women, whose language Thea especially was unhappy to learn was somewhat different from their teacher's, frustrated them. Each day they sat together working on their language, eager to talk to the women about Jesus. It made them neglect almost everything else. "It [the language] is difficult, but not impossible," she reported.[137] Now they were beginning to translate the Gospel of John into Chinese.

Their letters raised much concern at home. Every issue of *Kinamissionæren* contained letters from people representing newly organized groups whose main purpose it was to support the mission in China. "We girls here have in Jesus' Name established a society so we can, soon, with God's help, be able to send a little help to the China Mission," wrote a Mathilde Haugerud. Those at home had been made keenly aware by the letters of the missionaries of all the difficulties their brothers and sisters were facing in their proposed move to Fancheng. Even as they were finished with the compound in Hankow, they were beginning to plan their mission in

Fancheng. In his report to the annual meeting of the China Mission Society, President Oppegaard noted, with thanksgiving, that the members of the society had been more generous than the China Mission Society could have expected, so they as a society were able to support the new mission station the Rønnings were planning. In addition they were hoping to send out more missionaries in the next year. They also were planning to expand their group and supporters with help from the United Church, which had just suffered the breakup with the Friends of Augsburg in 1893. The attractions of the mission to the Malagasy that had come out of the Conference and Augsburg Seminary had been strong; it was made stronger by the 1890 merger of the Norwegian-Danish Augustana Synod, the Norwegian Danish Conference, and the Anti-Missourian Brotherhood into the United Church. This merger had been tempting to the Hauge Synod, but they could not see their way to an agreement, even though they were friendly with many in the new church. As the United Church gained strength, the leaders of the China Mission Society looked to many in the United Church (*Forenede*) to support their work in China, and many had.

Now the China Mission Society was able to turn their attention to other things such as increasing the number of members on the board and committees with people who came from other synods. In that regard Oppegaard had spoken with Pastor John A. Brynjulfsen (1853-1931) of the United Church, but he declined. Finally, he asked A. H. Lange of San Francisco, the man who had helped the Rønnings find their way around the city and brought them on board their ship. He agreed to help, which gave them more reach as a society, now even to the West Coast and San Francisco, where they needed someone to help as new missionaries began their journey across the Pacific and returned on furlough.

ESTABLISHING THE FANCHENG STATION

Halvor wrote to Østby on June 18, 1893, from Fancheng to tell how they were preparing to build the station there and the difficulties involved. Netland and Nelson had been there some weeks before and bought three lots where they could build their station, but as they began their work, the mandarin from whom they had bought the land began to pull away from the agreement and said that the Chinese man who had helped with the purchase had no right to sell Chinese land to foreigners. Neither Netland nor Nelson could make a successful argument, so they left for Hankow and the American consulate to see what could be done. Meanwhile their teacher, Ting, who was interested in Christianity and whom they expected to convert shortly, was arrested, suffered 400 blows, and was thrown into prison as was another Chinese helper. Halvor remarked with dismay about the unrighteousness of this event. Then he discovered that their contractor had not been able to pay his workers. It was so bad that he could not sleep. It exhausted Rønning, and he could not fully explain to his readers how bad it was, except that Mrs. Ting was weeping at his feet as he was writing the letter, pleading with him to get her husband released from jail, something he attempted but was unable to do. The lack of law and regulations in China, and the capricious cruelty of the magistrates, upset and shocked Halvor. On July 1, 1893, a new problem would emerge.

They heard the news that on July 1, 1893, two Swedish missionaries with the Swedish Missionary Society, Otto Frederick Wikholm (1861-1893) and Anders Daniel Johansen (1859-1893), had been cruelly murdered in Sungpu, Hubei province, by some Chinese bandits or rebels. It struck the Norwegians hard. Thea wrote that the mutilated bodies of the missionaries had been retrieved and their condition shocked her: Their whole bodies had been stuck with knives, their heads crushed. The only way to recognize them was by their teeth. They buried them on July 9. Thea used the old sentence,

"The blood of the martyrs is the seed of the church."[138] Not only the Swedish government but also other Western nations demanded that China punish the murderers and that the official, Zhang Zhidong, be demoted. The incident, known as the Sungpu Affair, affected much of their work during that year. Part of the problem was the negative reaction from the Chinese to the action by the Swedish government, forcing the national government to seek punishment for the murder of the Swedish men. Halvor felt they were resisting his efforts simply because of that issue.

The next morning Halvor was going to try one more time to get Ting released, then leave on a tour to the northern part of Hunan Province to see what other places would be appropriate for a station. He was longing for his family and hoped he would be home soon. He had been to the magistrate eight times, he wrote, with no success. Finally, he said, the man, who had read some of their literature, understood that "we were people of peace and came with good teachings." Part of the problem was trying to keep the official from "losing face." This important part of Chinese culture, new to them, frequently frustrated the missionaries until they came more fully to understand it. Finally, they came with a compromise concerning the property: They would not build too tall a building, with a roof like the Chinese roofs, and would move the garden some feet to one corner of the lot and promised to maintain and keep in good repair the flood walls around it. The compromise was written up, signed, and sent to the viceroy in Wuchang to be approved. It was a frustrating experience for Halvor and the others. He had been gone eleven weeks and saw very little relief in sight, but to give up the plans to establish the station in Fancheng felt to him, he wrote, like denying his call to do mission. "Old Adam, who followed me to China, is very unhappy and complains night and day how hard it is to have to go on a mission trip and live in an unhealthy hut during the hottest days of summer. But I tell him what an old layman said to me in Norway, 'Oh, that Old Adam, he has been made a minor.'"[139]

As Halvor was returning from Fancheng, Thea wrote to her family at home telling them about the health and situation of the missionaries. Many had been sick, Ludvig Johnson had died of dysentery, but the most distressing was that Mrs. Nyholm, from Denmark, had taken leave of her senses and had to go home by herself, leaving her husband in China until he got things ready. While this may have been more of a problem for the missionaries than they let on, we cannot tell. Thea was filled with sympathy for Nyholm. "O it is hard for brother Nyholm to see his wife lose her mind; there cannot be anything much worse."[140] Oline took her to Shanghai where she could get her on the boat home to Denmark. "It was too difficult for Nyholm to watch over her and get things ready before he could leave."[141]

Oline Hermanson at the same time was also discovering more about the situation of women in China. It was not encouraging to her. Millions of women were waiting to hear about Jesus, she wrote. "It's heart-rending to see how women are treated like slaves. Often they have cruel husbands, for whom she must earn money for drink—if she gives birth to a daughter, she is hated. They learn they have no souls, so it is no wonder that they kill themselves and their daughters."[142]

This issue was also addressed at the Columbian Exposition at Chicago that same year in the Women's Congress of Mission. Mrs. Schauffler, wife of Adolf F. Schauffler, whose Bible Missionary Training School in Cleveland, Ohio, trained missionaries to the Slavic immigrants in the United States, delivered the concluding address at the October 4, 1893, meeting. In it she argued that "women's work is a power for good in four ways: 1) in diffusing missionary information and forging a sympathetic personal link with workers in the fields, 2) in planning and carrying on specific work for women and children, 3) in promoting systematic giving in the churches and 4) in training the young in intelligent interest in mission."[143] While she was merely stating the obvious and something all the missionaries knew, it was important that it was so clearly put at this important event. Women missionaries were needed.

Mr. and Mrs. Nyholm

Establishing the Fancheng Station | 115

By September 4, 1893, Halvor had returned to Hankow. The difficulties with the magistrates and other officials continued. Now the mandarin wanted them to buy another lot next to the ones they had bought. Halvor would not do this. He wanted to return quickly to Fancheng to take the place of the Swedish missionaries who had been killed. "We must be ready to give our lives for the gospel. Remember it was on the dark Good Friday that the victory was won."[144] The Chinese authorities were wary of them after the murder of the missionaries and the demands made by the Swedes and other Western governments to find justice.

They were also angry with all Americans since the passage of what Halvor called the "unChristian" Geary Law in 1892, an extension and strengthening of the Chinese Exclusion Act of 1882. Halvor did not approve of the law. Its passage drove honest and hardworking heathens, he said, out of the "so-called Christian land of America."[145] His position on this was not unusual for the missionaries, who saw the consequences of such a law on the reputation of America, as well as what they saw as its injustice. In May of 1893, the Supreme Court upheld the law in a split decision, making the Chinese even angrier. Many refused to do business with American interests. In August 1893, the *Mission Review* reported that the Mission Union had passed a strong resolution protesting America's policy toward the Chinese in America, especially the Geary Law.[146]

Despite his frustration with the system, Halvor did understand some of the reasons for the reluctance of the Chinese to favor them. He was also glad to report that he had had two significant conversations with men of high standing, one who came to him like Nicodemus, by dark of night, disguised as a common laborer. "It was encouraging to experience the same things that Jesus did during his mission work on earth." He concluded by saying they would soon leave for Fancheng where, if they did not receive permission to build the house as they wanted, they would rent a place. The Lord would provide.

This time was also difficult for the mission because of the financial panic of 1893 which began in June of that year and, though the mission supporters were loyal, the effect of the panic on the farm as much as the city slowed the growth of many church organizations during this time, not least the mission movement. Although one hears very little of it in the religious papers, it is not difficult to imagine that the pressing nature of the needs in China and the lack of funds in America made the organizations think of merging. The magazine took pains to print little notes from all sorts of people who had sent in very minimal gifts, such as the letter from an old woman surviving on the Dakota prairie: "I'm sending in $2.00 for mission," hoping it would encourage others to do the same.[147] When one considers that the yearly salary of one female missionary was $300, such a gift would be as substantial then as a thousand dollars today.

All this time Thea and the other women with her were settling into their routines of learning the language, working with the women they met in their work, and writing home to their many supporters. Thea frequently corresponded with the Girls' Mission Society in Dawson, Minnesota, one of the most supportive groups in the Hauge Synod. After something of a sermon on the importance of doing the Lord's work in China, she told of their work with the language. She found it difficult to speak to and understand Chinese women with their slightly different dialect from the teacher and was frustrated that she would have to learn that language, too, if she were going to continue her mission among the women of China. Although she was improving, the work with the language was tedious and slow. She asked the girls in Dawson to pray that she would have patience to endure.

The best news was that they had been invited to the home of the teacher, Mr. Ma, for dinner, and then to visit the women's temple next to their home. They had gladly accepted the invitation, but were shocked by the temple, which celebrated the blessing, "May you be mother of a hundred sons, and the grandmother of a thousand." The sight of the Buddha grieved her. Her comment on the religion is of interest: "They say if they are not kind and do not serve this idol, they will receive a terrible punishment after they die. They know punishment, death and eternity, but no salvation."[148] She added that, after their visit to their teacher's home, she did know that the Chinese could be clean.

About that time Thea, Hannah, Oline, and Olava started a small circle for women and children which had met twice. Ten women and six children had come. "We sing for them, our teacher Tang reads something from the Bible and prays to God, and we talk privately with them about God and what had just been read. They ask many questions, and right in the middle of our talk, they might ask how much a piece of our clothing cost."[149] The inability of Chinese women to think abstractly about what was not right in front of them always surprised and sometimes irritated the missionaries, but these women they were teaching had no education and no practice in abstract thinking; they were like any people from a culture where there was no writing. They constantly surprised the missionaries with what they thought were strange questions.

Women missionaries: Mrs. Thea Landahl, Mrs. Gidske Himle, Mrs. Hanna Rønning, and Miss Marietta Fugleskjel

When the missionary women wearied of studying (one almost gets the picture of college girls or graduate students studying together for exams) they would take a walk out in the city around their station in order to be reminded of why they were studying so hard. On their walks they would see the dire conditions of the people who were now dreading the winter because they did not have clothes enough to keep them warm. "Their homes, their clothes, and everything witness to the fact that almost all sense for what is noble and good had disappeared in all this poverty." Even worse, they thought, were the lives of many "women who had never been outside of the walls of their homes. Never had they seen God's beautiful creation and never have thought of our dear Father who created heaven and earth."[150]

While the missionaries watched the Chinese political situation with interest, the goings on at court were remote for them, as they were for most Chinese. By 1894, the Empress Dowager Cixi was getting ready to celebrate her sixtieth birthday in 1895. The missionaries wondered if the spirit of Christ was changing China when they heard that she had told the mandarins who would ordinarily have sent her lavish gifts not to spend money on such presents, but rather to use the money to help the poor. That amounted to something like $20,000 dollars per province, one source estimated. Was this a hint that change was working its way through the Chinese system? The missionaries hoped so.[151]

As the year 1893 came to an end, the legal matters surrounding the mission's right to build a house in Fancheng came to a head. The missionaries had appealed to the Treaty of Shanxi, Article XII, which said that "British subjects, whether at the ports or other places, desiring to build and open houses, warehouses, churches, hospitals or burial grounds shall make their agreement for the land and buildings they require at the rates prevailing amongst the people." Americans could use the same law because they fit under the "most favored nations" clause of the treaty. Halvor noted that even though it was in their favor, the mandarins had begun to trample the treaty under their feet and would not allow missionaries to work in the country. Governor Zhang Zhidong of Hubei Province seemed to be the worst of all. They hoped that the consulates of other countries in Beijing would be

Empress Dowager Cixi

successful in their appeals to the national government. Halvor left it in God's hands. The major problem, however, was that the government was so corrupt and its powers so weak, it was difficult to make an agreement that would be recognized throughout the country. News traveled rather slowly between the capital and the provinces, and the local magistrates used that to their advantage. Only the Americans' connection to the legation in Beijing could resolve some of their problems. Having the support now of the vice-consul of the United States in Beijing, they hoped that, with a little patience, it would work out. To that end, Netland and Halvor planned to return to Fancheng after Christmas to complete the negotiations and to lay the plans for a station there. Netland, now a widower, had the luxury of being able to leave his two-month-old baby with the "sisters," as he called them—Thea, Olava, Oline, Hannah, and Mrs. Nelson.

Olava Hodnefield wrote a long letter describing their 1893 Christmas in the compound with the Chinese children who sang in Chinese and recited the Lord's Prayer and Bible verses from their classes, after which they went into the dining room for the Christmas Eve festivities with presents and food. The Norwegian children sang "Thy Little Ones, Dear Lord Are We," among others. It was an evening like none other, she exclaimed. To celebrate Christmas, the birth of the Christ child among those who had never before heard of Jesus' birth was very moving. In addition, the entire group was much aware that their sister, Berthine Netland, who had died December 8, 1893, was now celebrating Christmas in heaven, something that both grieved them and cheered them. They did not grieve as those without hope, they remarked frequently.

Olava Hodnefield

Olava and Thea, over the year since Olava's arrival the January of 1893, had developed a close friendship and were beginning to enjoy their work with the Chinese. For Christmas Halvor had given them each $1.00 and told them to spend it as they liked, warning them against going out on the streets where they would be sorely tempted to give it away. They, of course, did go out, whereupon they were invited into the room of an old woman who was dying, in a house where the wind, rain, and sun had free entrance through both ceiling and walls. As they told her of Jesus, she could not believe their story of a living God who loved her enough to die for her. Where was he, she asked. When they told her again that God loved her, she was amazed to think a god could care for a woman. Thea gave her fifty cents and prayed for her. They left her and immediately met a couple in distress who had nothing for a home but a little hole in the city wall. They were soon relieved of the rest of their money.[152]

The war with Japan was about to begin, and it made it more and more difficult for missionaries in China, because much of the rage against the system was directed at them. Hannah had written that many of the missionaries, fearful of what might happen, were thinking of escaping to Shanghai.[153] Sun Yatsen, the founder of modern China, had organized the first of the secret societies he would use in his revolutionary struggles. Halvor had commented that the missionaries who had been around for a long while were hoping that there would be a war. Something was needed to knock sense into the people, especially the ruling classes, the missionaries said.[154] They complained about the Chinese notion that China was the Middle Kingdom, the central kingdom in the world. A defeat in battle, the missionaries argued, would surely change their image of themselves as invincible. When the defeat of the Chinese came on April 17, 1895, it did deeply disturb the Chinese sense of cultural superiority, but it did very little to benefit Christian missionary enterprise.

Sun Yatsen and wife Song Quinling

When Netland and Halvor left for Fancheng on January 9, 1894, they hoped to rent a house there, since the legal matters did not seem to be resolving in their favor. They left with only their hope and the advice of older missionaries that things would be resolved, so the group could move there in the spring. Netland, who became one of the best correspondents of the missionaries, wrote about his own health and his need for rest and restoration. He was now strong and healthy, he said, and could travel with Rønning, grateful that Thea was able to care for the baby. She apparently was a great favorite of the missionary children. As a single woman missionary her duties were frequently double: not only did she have to do the professional work of a teacher, she was also expected to do women's

Establishing the Fancheng Station | 121

work in the compound. Netland commended her loving care for the children, even as he bitterly lamented his sorry state at being alone in China with his child. "How it crushes me when I think that I am homeless, lonesome, and abandoned. Though it could be worse than it is. I live among friends and acquaintances and God is powerful to heal all my hurts."[155] It was not long before he married Oline Hermanson.

These vignettes give us a picture of marriage on the mission field. Some missions absolutely forbade single men from becoming missionaries, though single women were allowed. The Hauge Synod and China Mission Society had no such rule. Thea, Halvor, and Hannah, the first three missionaries they sent out, were unmarried, facts no one mentioned in the publications. What was said in private may have been quite different, but we know nothing of that now. Unmarried women were paid $350 a year and unmarried men $400, an injustice no one really remarked on in the press, though it may have riled some women missionaries in the Hauge Synod. They were all provided travel, language instruction, and a free house. A married couple—and there were always two missionaries in a couple—received $600 a year. The work of the single woman missionary may have been more demanding than that of the men, if one can judge from the action of the Mission Society in June 1894, to send enough money to let the missionaries hire a woman to help with the housework. This was to give Thea Rønning and Olava Hodnefield more time to study the language intensely and get some free time. Thea had become quite ill not long after she took over the care of the Netland baby. She had gotten a bad cold, with no relief. Hannah wrote to inform their readers of her illness and tell more about their common life. She had not been quite as faithful a correspondent since the birth of her two young boys, but now she took a moment to write.

Norah Nelson

In this letter she told a gripping story common to all missionaries at the time: describing what it was like when the Nelsons sent their oldest daughter, Norah, to school in Qufu. "At the boat we had a short time of prayer; Mr. and Mrs. Nelson knelt by the side of their daughter, and with pain in their prayer and tears sent her away. The separation was heavy when we left America; and no less heavy here in China, where life's comforts can be found only in our own home."[156]

Thea's illness may have been bronchitis, pleurisy or pneumonia, but we are not sure. Halvor thanked a group at home for sending Thea stockings, a gift for which she was grateful, he wrote, but too sick to write a letter expressing her gratitude.[157] At the end of her letter, Hannah reported that they were soon leaving for Fancheng, and although she enjoyed very much the times they had had together in Hankow, she was eager to begin the work there.

In Fancheng they were hoping that the Sungpu Affair, in which the European powers held the Chinese responsible for the death of the Swedish missionaries, had made the Chinese more willing to negotiate. In any case, Netland concluded that something had to happen soon in China so it not only would become more favorable to the gospel, but also become a land where the law was not so capricious and personal. "Mission life is a life in battle and tears and victory, both private and public," he concluded. "After rain, comes the sunshine."[158]

On February 5, 1894, Daniel Nelson, who in many ways was the leader of the group since he had been there the longest, received a telegram from Netland and Halvor announcing that they had rented a house and were beginning to repair and upgrade it so the group could live there in comfort. The case had now reached the attention of the American minister, Colonel Charles Denby, who wanted to know whether they were an American or Norwegian group, given their name, Norwegian American Mission. Things moved slowly on, while the men worked in Fancheng.

By this time, the women's Chinese was good enough for them to use it to tell Chinese women the gospel in the simplest way. Oline Hermanson described one of their first visits in the neighborhood. Using the money they had gotten for Christmas from Halvor, they had gone together to buy clothes and rice to give to the neediest around them. Warned by their teacher not to carry materials that could be seen, for fear of robbers, they hid some under their coats and prayed that they would find someone to give to. Soon they found a poor sick woman who had to use crutches to get around. Her home was a small bamboo hut with a bed of straw and a small grill to cook her rice. When she invited them in, they were happy to accept the invitation. As they spoke about the living God, she was unable to understand and told them her eyes were so bad she could not see God. As Oline explained to her about God, she exclaimed that it was amazing to hear that a God could think about her. When they gave her their gifts she was overwhelmed. Thank our God, they said, not us, which she promised to do. When they came back on their way home from this adventure, they were surprised to see her in a neighbor's house telling them all that had happened to her and about the God that had sent them to her. Those listening to her, when they saw the women, surrounded them and made them hurry home before anything happened. All told, they were grateful to God for the chance they had had to witness to God's love and to give something to the poor woman.[159]

About the same time, things in Fancheng had finally been settled. At first when they arrived the way forward did not seem promising. They had found a house that seemed very appropriate and arranged to rent it, but the owner did not appear at the time they had expected. It seemed that all landlords in the city were afraid to rent to Westerners. They were certain that the magistrate had secretly told the owner not to rent his place to them. They had not brought with them the proper paperwork. Before they could rent the house, their teacher said, they should have the paper in hand and show it to the man. During this stressful time, they were frequently on their knees in prayer. They finally had the teacher write a document with each point clearly stated as to what they would do and what they expected from the Chinese. After they made four copies and secured a gift for the official, they sent their proposal with a messenger. He wanted to speak directly with them, so they rented a rickshaw and went to speak with him. They found him to be interested in their case, and he said he could not receive the gift, for people would speak badly of him. They also asked that their helper, Ting, would be set free from prison where he had now languished over almost a year.

As soon as they had the official permission to rent a house, Halvor and Netland began to repair it, working the next weeks to make it ready for their small band of family and colleagues. They were thankful that it lay only a stone's throw from the lot they had purchased and that it was dry and airy, a good thing in a place where malaria was endemic. In a few days they would leave for Hankow to prepare to move the group. On their way home on the boat, Halvor wrote they had left March 9, 1894, and everything had finally gone well. The magistrate had given them permission to do as they had hoped they could do, and Ting, the imprisoned teacher, had been set free. For that they had much for which to be thankful. They were also hearing that the Sungpu Affair had not been handled to the satisfaction of other Western powers and that it was being taken up again in Beijing. Once again, Halvor concluded, the blood of the martyrs is the seed of the church. Since he could not send the letter until he had arrived home on March 15, 1894, he was able to add that Thea was better. In addition he thanked the Willing Workers at home for sending them money to care for two small girls the missionaries had taken in. Not long afterward, Halvor, with great relief, reported that the local magistrate had finally issued a proclamation that all should know that these men from the West were teachers of peace and would teach people their doctrines of peace. No one, the proclamation continued, should think, speak, or act against the missionaries or oppose them. This was reason to thank the magistrate who had in the eleventh hour given them the permission to do what they felt called to do. In addition, Mr. Ting, was now recovering from his imprisonment, although he had been severely mistreated there, so much so that it took him some time to heal.[160]

Thea wrote to her parents and siblings on March 5, 1894, while Netland and Halvor were in Fancheng, that she now was well enough to write letters, something her doctor had forbidden her to do for two months if she wanted to get well. If her health did not improve, he had said, she would have to go home. She reflected on the warning all the missionaries dreaded, after the efforts they had put into learning the difficult language. So she followed his instructions, partly because she realized her mission to China would be ended if she had to go home or if she died—a warning they had received from veteran missionaries who had seen far too many of their kind come to China and fail because they had not kept their health.

Her diagnosis had been *"bryst-sygdomen"* which today would mean breast cancer. In her day it probably meant pleurisy or pneumonia since her doctor's advice that she rest completely for two months appeared to have been the correct treatment. Since she was writing to her family, she also took the occasion to report on the rest of the family's health: Hannah, who had been ill, had improved, and Nilius, the oldest child of Halvor, was beginning to walk and loved to go outdoors. Hannah was now sewing him new pants before his father returned. Then she added, "Little Sigfrid Netland is healthy and is doing very well. I have no interest in writing more." [161] What did she mean by this comment? This is the kind of comment, given the circumstances, that can only intrigue the historian. Was she aware that Netland was courting Oline and would marry her before they left for Fancheng on April 28? It is rather like her failure to comment after Halvor and Hannah married. Was something disturbing her? It is impossible to tell, but the hints are tantalizing.

The China Thea Experienced

Market in Hankow, 1890

Working the land
near the mission station

Market in Hankow, 1890

Missionaries with Hudson Taylor

The door to a Chinese home

Chinese teacher with
his wife and family

GETTING ORGANIZED AT HOME AND IN CHINA

About this same time, as they were making ready to move to Fancheng, trouble was brewing at home among their supporters in the Hauge Synod. It could have been predicted. When the young pastors had bolted the Hauge Synod annual meeting to begin the Norwegian-American China Mission Society, their urgency, while commendable, had understandably ruffled feathers among the leadership—probably the more responsible or at least the organizationally savvy members of the older generation. Over time other groups, not only the Hauge Synod, had come to support them. Of course, the mission society of the Hauge Synod was behind them, but the relationship became confused. It meant also that the supporters of the China mission in the Hauge Synod were overworked in regard to that good cause.

To deal with the problem, the Hauge Synod Board of Missions, at a meeting in Kenyon, Minnesota, February 24-26, 1894, decided to present the Hauge Synod annual meeting a resolution to offer the China Mission Society something of a buyout: They would take over the society completely, edit and publish the magazine *China Missionary*, as well as elect a separate board of the Hauge Synod to oversee the mission. Halvor responded to the issue with distress. "Why should the China Mission (its missionaries) be ordered from back home so that all Norwegian American Lutheran Christians can stand together?" For him and for most missionaries around the world, the ecumenical question of how Christians could work together on the mission field was far more important than theological or denominational debates. "For the sake of the salvation of the heathen we pray that you will take care for each other and do everything possible to avoid splitting hearts," he pleaded. He suggested that they have an extra meeting of the two parties after the Hauge

Synod annual meeting, when they could establish a synod society, like the organization for the mission to the Jews, Zion Society for Israel (*Zionsforeningen*).[162]

Rønning family in Chinese dress

Before the Rønning group left for Fancheng on March 26, 1894, they had the first meeting of the Norwegian-American Lutheran Mission in China. Their deliberations were published in *Kinamissionæren*, and they show the seriousness and maybe the officiousness of these young missionaries. The conference included the eight missionaries: Mr. and Mrs. Rønning, Mr. and Mrs. Daniel Nelson, Misses Hodnefield, Thea Rønning, and Hermanson, and Mr. Netland. Halvor was elected chairman and Netland the secretary. They took up many questions such as who should go to Fancheng—the Rønnings, Miss Hodnefield, Netland, and Miss Hermanson; how much married and unmarried missionaries should receive for their necessities. They also decided that the missionaries had to work in concert with God's Word and the Lutheran Confessions; that Miss Rønning and Miss Hodnefield could engage a Chinese woman to help them with their mission work; and that they could, on their own, determine her pay; etc. An interesting resolution was passed on April 18 at a later meeting, probably as a result of informal conversations among them, which determined who had the right to vote: the solution was that men who had been on the field for a year had voting rights, women could speak at the conference and had voting rights on issues that had to do with women's issues in their work. (The question of women's right to vote both in civic elections and in the congregation was beginning to rage at home, and not surprisingly it was the pietists—perhaps from their acquaintance with Hauge and the notion that spiritual gifts were what qualified one for a call, not one's gender—who tended to be more liberal on this than the more orthodox. Trinity congregation in Minneapolis had given women the vote in 1892, although not the right to speak.) The meeting appears to have been rather formal, but it did put the questions before them into a structured conversation that expedited their work. We can see this in the resolutions they passed at this meeting:

Resolved: 1) that the missionaries be given a sabbatical every seven years; 2) that a missionary should learn the language in three years (although the consequences of their not learning the language are not described, it gave them the possibility to send home a candidate who would be a drag on their energies); 3) that their supporting groups in America had made things more complicated for them by sending money from two different organizations to do essentially the same thing, build an orphanage; 4) that they would use the Griffith John translation of the Bible into Chinese for their mission work; and finally, 5) that they would meet the next May in Fancheng.[163]

In the previous issue of *Kinamissionæren*, Thea had written an edifying letter to the Hauge congregation's Ladies Aid in Faribault, Minnesota. Despite her loneliness for the group and her good memories of the times they had spent together, now after two years in China she could say that she was glad to be where she was, even though there had been much loss and sorrow among their group. She regretted most especially the death of Mrs. Netland, with whom she had spent two wonderful years in the mission compound in Hankow, working on their Chinese. Apparently Mrs. Netland had died of blood poisoning after giving birth, not uncommon during childbirth. Watching her die had been a difficult experience for Thea, who had been present at her death struggles.[164] Except for a few other news notes, the rest of the letter is a typical document of the pietists, in which letters served as a kind of edification for the receiver, rather on the model of Paul's letters to his congregations. They are almost a literary genre in the form of Paul's letter to the Colossians, filled with greetings, references to favorite Bible passages, and encouragement to the audience to continue in the faith with a few details from the writer's experiences at the time. The urgency of their cause—bringing the gospel to the Chinese before it was too late—was foremost in her mind. Anyone wanting to hear extensive reports on what they were doing, what they were eating or wearing, will be disappointed, but these letters were as much for strengthening their reader spiritually as they were for anything else. Her audience was the women's groups who, like the ancient church, gathered to hear these letters read. We can see them in the home of one of their number listening to the letter from their dear friend as they sat around at their meetings darning socks and sewing for the cause of mission, and then resolving to do more for her. It was an excellent way to garner support, and the women writing in China knew it was an important part of their vocation.

Cover of *Kinamissionæren*

There was about a three-month delay from the writing to the publication of the letters in the magazine. While they knew, for example, that the missionaries were moving to Fancheng about the time they were meeting, they would have to wait some months before they would get the details from another letter. Because they had given money to build the home in Hankow and now to establish a station in Fancheng, they had real interest in how their gifts had borne fruit. The missionaries knew how vital such communications were and tried to take time for such correspondence so the people at home would be able to follow their progress. Both Halvor and Thea wrote, while they were waiting for their boat to leave Hankow

Getting Organized | 131

for Fancheng, on April 28, 1894, that they had all their goods on board a boat and were waiting for the weather and the Han River to recede a bit, given the spring run-off, which Thea said had been so great that several hundred boats had been destroyed and many hundreds of people drowned. A journey upstream, against the current, was not easy, and they needed to observe carefully the conditions of the river before departing. As usual, they were confident, however, that God was with them. Halvor in a parenthetical phrase added something Thea said nothing about: that Netland had just married Oline Hermanson. "It was necessary before the trip to Fancheng, and we had to leave before the heat began. Netland had to do it for the sake of his child, or else he would have had to go home. I am therefore glad for that."[165] He then turned to official matters of their first meeting as an organization in China which were reported in this later issue.[166]

Why Thea did not say a word about the marriage of her good friend Oline to Netland when her brother did is not clear to us. She had been given the care of Netland's daughter after the death of Mrs. Berthine Netland, and she had flourished under her care, something Netland himself praised her for. Soon after that, however, Thea had become ill, probably because of her overwork. It may be that Oline then took the child, but nothing in the record tells us that. Was Thea upset that she was not chosen by Netland? Did she not like him, so she was not upset? For Halvor the marriage was clearly in every sense a marriage of convenience. The baby was apparently thriving. From the records available we have no clue about Thea's feelings on the issue.

The trip up the Han River, about 400 miles, took them twenty-six days. Thea's description of the trip up river helps us visualize what it was like in Old China. The boat was almost seventy-five feet long and fifteen feet wide. It was of the best design, but still the rain, which was nearly constant at that time, got into their cabins. The boat was powered by wind when the winds were in their favor, but in this case they were not, so they needed men on the shore pulling the boat against the current by ropes tied around the mast. When there was an especially strong headwind, they had to stop and wait until the wind changed. So the trip was slow, leisurely, one might say, except for the discomforts of the rain and the roiling of the water, which was dangerous to anyone who fell into it. While the boat was large enough for them to walk about, if it was wet it would be easy to slip off the deck into the water. To their grief, it happened to their party when the boy, Sun Wang, whom they had taken with them to help as they made their home in the new city, fell out of the boat and drowned in the river. Because it had been dark when he fell in, they only heard his cries, but could not see to save him. Halvor would later describe their efforts to rescue the boy, just to the point of jumping into the river to find him, from which he was restrained by the others who told him he could never swim in the raging Han River. All of them, including Daniel Nelson, expressed their grief over the loss of the young boy.[167] Halvor spoke of the death of Sun Wang like that of losing a dear younger brother. Although the boy had not been baptized, Halvor hoped that because of his interest and profession of faith the young man was in heaven.

Both Halvor and Netland later gave more details of their trip up the river and the dangers they encountered on the way. They had been warned about robbers who prowled the river banks looking for hostages and rich victims whom they could rob. A perilous event happened to the missionaries while they were docked in Shouyun because of rain and strong head winds. A woman began shrieking on the dock and said they had taken her son, a common accusation against foreign devils.[168] The uproar was both frightening and strange to them. A crowd gathered quickly, something they had seen happening many times before; they knew the dangers of a mob which could not be controlled. They pressed toward the boat to board it and search for the child, which looked to be very threatening to the missionaries. They knew of situations like this which had quickly deteriorated into chaos. Fortunately, the captain of the boat and his crew stood between them and the mob, probably saving their lives. Soon a mandarin on the river also came to them and helped still the uproar, for which Halvor and the entire group were grateful.

After about a month, the small group arrived in Fancheng and began their work building the compound and establishing themselves in the city. They were all pleased by the warm greetings the Chinese had given them upon their arrival. On June 2, 1894, they had all been invited to their neighbor's home for his seventieth birthday party. The celebrations lasted through the day and included two meals which they enjoyed, even to the point of using chopsticks. Halvor did allow, however, that this hospitality, while encouraging, would not necessarily result in conversions, although it did give them a good feeling to have such a warm welcome from the neighbors.[169] Thea in a letter to her family in Norway gave them details of Halvor's family, and Nilius Rønning, who now had a Chinese babysitter. He had enjoyed the boat ride and all the people around him. He was thriving, she said, and then commented on how nice the new site for the house in Fancheng was: "Here nature is very beautiful and the house is high enough but close to the river so that it looks rather Norwegian in its aspect, with the river and the mountains around us." She concluded with the postscript that Halvor had bought a cow so they could get fresh milk.[170]

The conflicts back home between their supporters in the China Mission Society and the Hauge Synod were escalating and became more and more troubling to them. One of the issues was the wish of many in the newly formed United Church to support their mission, and the China Mission Society seemed to be the better way since it did not involve supporting the Hauge Synod. In a letter written on April 28, 1894, the six missionaries regretted that those at home were in conflict while they in China were facing the need of millions of heathen people. Their hope was that somehow the society and the organization would find a way to work together. They wished that the United Church could be active members of the China Mission Society, especially after their annual meeting. While it was regrettable, they did agree that many in the church who had done much for the China Mission Society should continue to do so and that in the next year these issues would be dealt with for the good of the mission. The letter was signed by Halvor and Hannah Rønning, Olava Hodnefield, Thea Rønning, Sigvald and Oline Netland. Thea, Halvor, and Hannah would later commit themselves to serving and relating officially to the Hauge Synod, and soon after their letters and reports went directly to the Synod and its papers, especially *Budbæreren*, the paper of the Hauge Synod.[171]

The July 15, 1894, issue of *Kinamissionæren* reported that at the Hauge Synod annual meeting a new plan for the support of the mission had been discussed to assure the continuing work of the China mission. They passed the resolution of the Board of Mission that the Hauge Synod should take over the China Mission Society and the original be disbanded so the work of the China mission would be more efficiently funded. To that end the synod selected a board to run the mission: Østby and Martin Gustav Hanson for a three year term, Christoffer O. Brøhaugh (1841-1908) and Oppegaard for two years, J. A. Gunning, Arne Ellerdson Boyum (1833-1913), and O. S. Haugen for one-year terms. In their organization:

> they voted M. G. Hanson as chairman, Oppegaard as vice-chairman, and Østby as secretary, and Haugen as treasurer. The United Church voted that they were agreed that the United Church would send its contributions to the China Mission of the Hauge Synod's Mission treasury and the Hauge Synod send its contributions to the Malagasy Mission treasury until further work can help with their common work.[172]

This seemed to be a sensible solution for the time being, meaning that the Hauge Synod members could contribute to missionaries in Madagascar and the United Church to the China mission without having to duplicate organizational efforts. The issues would receive more specific attention at the general meeting of the mission society at Our Savior's congregation in Inwood, Iowa, October 9-11, 1894. They would decide at the meeting whether or not the society would accept the invitation of the Hauge Synod to give over all their work to the synod.[173] The missionaries waited with great interest to hear how the meeting went, after their first month of moving into the new dwelling, which they did before the terrible heat of summer overcame them.

As they had come to expect, sickness stalked them through the time of heat. Netland and Oline had both been sick partly because of the "terrible" heat which took their strength and energy from them. While they do not say what illness they had suffered, they all told of how difficult it was to be sick in such heat. It could almost bring on a heat stroke by itself with temperature never below 100 degrees F in the house and over 120 outside in the sun. Whether or not they were ill, they were somewhat laid low by it since it was so enervating to them, these "children from the north," as they described themselves. Nothing much got done, although they made plans for their work when the heat subsided. From the first they planned to open a school for boys in Fancheng, but not during the two hottest months of the year, July and August.[174] To their surprise and joy, girls also wanted to come to the school which was free. To meet with their requests, they included both boys and girls in their classes. Many of the children became interested enough in their teachings to return for Sunday school. This success made them feel hopeful about the progress of their work. In order to serve the Chinese better and attract them to the station, they knew that opening a clinic would do wonders. Netland had begun working as a doctor, meeting with the sick in the mornings. He began to regret that he had not trained as a doctor, because a doctor would be able to have twice as much effect with the Chinese, able to minister to both body and soul. It would not be long before a missionary with medical training, Thorstein Himle who had already met with the Rønnings in Faribault, would arrive.[175]

On August 8, 1894, Halvor wrote a long letter explaining what they had accomplished since they had arrived: "Oppressive heat in China these past days. The sweat runs both night and day, and these children of the North have panted for breath in this stuffy, burning air." He thought the temperature was 125 out in the sun and 100 in their rooms. In the winter it was also almost as cold as in Minnesota. In the summer, he explained they had monsoons from the south, and in winter the weather came from the north. This year, he said, the farmers were expecting a good crop because the *"feng shui"* was right. He then went on to explain how the mission work was going. Although they had prepared the house for themselves, there was still much to do to make the building appropriate for the teachers and servants they had in their employ, plus a large room for gatherings and a school yard, along with rooms for Chinese guests. Their first Sunday school sessions had been filled to overflowing, partly because of the typical curiosity of the Chinese, but still he thought they would have to expand the chapel immediately.

Halvor had noted on August 8, 1894, once again, "The women have been talking about how painful it was that parents had no interest in girl children and how difficult it is to give them an education. We prayed about it. Yesterday two girls came and knocked on our door asking for an education, today two more."[176] Although the women had been teaching the girls and meeting with the women who came to the station, more and more they felt the need to do something that could help the Chinese women around them immediately. Now they were insisting to their male colleagues that something needed to be done. Halvor wrote on November 15, 1894, that "our women have complained about how painful it is to see how little the Chinese care about their daughters."[177] It was an important concern among their supporters back home. They needed more workers to help with this mission.

On December 8, 1894, *Budbæreren* announced that the Hauge Synod had decided to call Miss Marietta Fugleskjel to the work in China. Her autobiography, printed in the same issue, told of her studies at St. Olaf and her ten years of teaching in common schools. "I want to help the poor heathen," she wrote, "and especially the poor Chinese women."[178] In addition to her preparation in teaching, she was making an effort to find some medical training before leaving because she was keenly aware that the mission work was much more effective when coupled with care for the physical body as well as the soul.[179]

Marietta Fugleskjel

This move received support from the members of the Hauge Synod partly because of the work of the magazine. Beginning with its June 1, 1894, issue, *Kinamissionæren* had published a series of articles on the place of women in China. The usual descriptions of foot binding and the notion that women had no souls in Chinese folk religion were included. The series ended with an appeal for Christian women at home to see the need and send help to their unbelieving and needy sisters in China.[180] This appeal to be sisterly was also an effective tool for raising money, and it worked to increase the efforts of the women at home. Hannah Rønning, who later became president of the Hauge Synod's Mission Dove Society, noted this in her speech to the first meeting of the Hauge Synod Mission Dove Society in 1901, clearly reminding the women of the organization that, though their first duties were in the home, they also were required by the gospel to meet the needs of the sisters across the sea. The Rønnings had taken in children who were left with them, and they were constantly refusing to buy children from distraught parents who could not support them and who were starv-

Getting Organized | 137

ing themselves. It distressed the missionaries not to be able to take those children, but rumor spread that the missionaries were buying Chinese children for cruel purposes, such as crushing their eyes for the silver in them. For that reason the Rønnings never would buy a child, though they did reach out to as many of them as they could. Not surprisingly the condition of women grew worse in times of famine and war, so the time of the Sino-Japanese War, from August 1, 1894, to April 17, 1895, was especially difficult.

One hears little from the missionaries during the high summer simply because of the heat. As Thea wrote her family, the reason she had not written since June was the extreme heat. It was impossible for her to do anything, she said, but move from one chair to another. While everyone was well, they were staying quiet. She did have the sad news to report that Norah Nelson had died while at school in Qufu, far from her parents. A most touching article in the following issue of the paper was the letter from the headmistress where Norah had died. Even at this distance it is almost unbearable. Norah had already distinguished herself among the missionaries for her diligence and sweet spirit, which she exhibited also in her school and in her death, which the headmistress had also marked. The cause of her death was not clear to them; Thea thought maybe dysentery or a stomach infection, an imprecise diagnosis that makes those of us who read these letters uncertain as to what the actual illness was. God was good to both give and take, she concluded. Then for the very first time in her letters Thea talks about gifts she has sent back to them—silk ribbons, chokers we might call them. Since they were not at all expensive she could send any other colors they wanted.[181] Earthly things had not seemed to interest Thea much in her previous letters; that she was thinking of gifts to send her family from China shows her to be more and more acquainted with and fond of China. Although hostilities between China and Japan were beginning, she writes little about it in these letters.

While these things were going on, the home front was also "at war." When the China Mission Society met at Inwood, Iowa, a town near Sioux City October 9-11, 1894, it voted, with thirty members present, not to accept the Synod's proposal and continue as it had. The next month the Hauge Synod's China Mission Society met and voted to cut all its informal ties with the China Mission Society and authorized their board to negotiate with the Society about their joint properties in China. They voted also to call missionaries of their own: Thorstein Himle and his wife, Gidske; Carl Landahl; and Marietta Fugleskjel. In addition they hired a traveling secretary who would gather support for the mission and called J. M. J. Hotvedt, a student at Red Wing Seminary, to be a medical missionary. They also resolved to canvas the missionaries in China—Halvor, Hannah, and Thea—about which organization they wanted to belong to and receive support from.

In August 1894, the war between Japan and China over Korea finally broke out. Difficulties between the two nations had been simmering for some time. The assassination of Kim Ok-gyun, a pro-Japanese Korean revolutionary, in Shanghai on March 28, 1894, made hostilities almost certain. Kim had been involved in a coup attempt in Korea in 1884 and had fled to Japan; the Japanese had turned down Korean demands that he be extradited. He was lured to Shanghai where he was killed by a fellow Korean, an action which made war almost impossible to avoid. War between China and Japan was officially declared on August 1, 1894. Thea had watched 1,500 soldiers marching out from Fancheng to Beijing which she noted was near Korea. Could China possibly lose to a smaller country, she wondered, as did many at the time. China had, even in its decline, a proud sense of its being the Middle Kingdom; its great size and population should have made it possible for China to defend against the much smaller country of Japan. However, Japan prevailed. The Qing Dynasty, led by Empress Dowager Cixi seemed to be on its last legs and was defeated, mostly because it had neither the capacity to unite the Chinese nor the materiel to fight a modern war. In 1894, when Japan declared war, the Empress Cixi was getting ready for the celebration of her sixtieth birthday. Although rumors, even today, argue that the empress did not understand the seriousness of the war because she insisted on using the money intended for the military to restore the Summer Palace, her dwelling, against the advice of her chancellors, other historians argue that she was more prudent than that. Still, she used money intended for the navy to restore an extravagant marble boat, which may have assured China's defeat in the war.

The near collapse of the dynasty was surely responsible for the failure of the local magistrates to respond quickly to the edicts from Beijing. The missionaries were more and more convinced that the regime needed to collapse in order for a new one to arise and begin to govern the country. Halvor also reported on the soldiers marching through the city and the fear it had engendered in them. Even if combat was far away, it made them anxious since both food and money were needed at the front. The needs of the military depleted the resources of the ordinary Chinese, so all were anxious about their survival. [182]

At this same time, Halvor also seconded Netland's wish for a better trained doctor and repeated his call for a medical missionary. Because the Chinese had heard that missionaries were very good doctors, they lined up outside the station simply to be treated by the missionaries, no matter how much they protested that they were not doctors. The missionaries had by now used up the medicine they had gotten for their own use and were reading in medical books about how to treat the many very common diseases endemic to China. People came to them for every reason, curiosity not the least, but they had heard something about the Christian God from others around them, especially the skill of the missionaries in being able to treat many illnesses (probably by ordering them to clean up and rest).

Netland gave a moving account of how a young woman, during the terrible heat of July 1894, had been brought to them on a wheelbarrow over several miles of primitive roads to receive treatment for what he thought was pneumonia, so bad she could scarcely breathe. After he gave her medicine (what kind he does not say), she seemed to rally. Oline Netland cradled her in her arms and soon she felt better. Because they had no room to keep her overnight, she went to a place nearby, but returned some days later in relapse. Once again he gave her the medicine and she seemed to rally and went home, thankful for their help. It was clear to him that if he would help them, they would, as they said, spread his name and his faith around their region. For him medical missionaries had two ways to preach, and he thought it important to see if they could, as a mission, employ medical

Oline Hermanson Netland

personnel as part of their mission. The Chinese wanted to find out who their God was and why the missionaries were establishing free schools for their children, in addition to having meetings for everyone in their church.[183]

THE WOMEN'S WORK TAKES HOLD

The women's Chinese had improved enough so they could make more visits to Chinese women in their homes. Thea was especially well regarded for her home visits to the women they were helping at the station. On October 11, 1894, after nine months of Chinese studies, Miss Hodnefield was able to accompany Thea in her visits to the women in their homes. They would not work directly with women without first visiting them in their homes.

Although Olava despaired of learning the language, she was happy to report that they had rented a house for their work with women. By November 1, they would have a girls' school. Already there were nine to ten students.[184] Olava also described the work they had to do to open the school and the complications of learning the "difficult language, so much so that I must ask myself sometimes whether I can be a blessing here for these people." They had finally found a house for the school for girls, but what they needed most from their supporters was prayer. "Pray for us!" she concluded.[185] The women worked hard to communicate with their servants and others around them to provide daily bread for the people in the station. In fact, they considered their helpers and servants to be their first mission field. Oline was amused to hear their cook, whom they thought would convert, say that he had seen them wash up and how clean they wanted things to be that "God is all about cleanliness and cannot bear dirt!"[186]

Thea, just thirty, was becoming more and more comfortable in China, even to the point of having fun, something she had hardly shown before. In describing a trip on the river, she told how she and Sister Caroline, a Danish deaconess, had gotten out of the boat and walked along the path beside the river for a while, probably where the boatmen walked when pulling the boats upstream. It was a lovely place, she said, and when men came to carry them in a sedan chair, Sister Caroline refused their help and took off her shoes and stockings and waded in the river, as did Thea, even though, according to Thea, they looked a sight.[187] It is a charming, and new, picture of these young women enjoying their lives in China and feeling at home.

Sister Caroline Johnson

The letters now were giving the supporters of the mission a close and specific sense, not only of the missionaries, but also of the Chinese people whom the missionaries were serving, as well as the larger geopolitical situation of China and other world matters having to do with the Far East. Hannah Rønning, in a letter from October 31, 1894, lamented the situation in China now that the war was making it more and more difficult for the work of the missionaries. Some were suggesting they go to Shanghai to be safer, but at the moment, she wrote, they were in a peaceful situation which meant, for her, that God was at work among them. Once again she reiterated the almost constant refrain among the missionaries that maybe the situation could open up the way for the gospel among the Chinese.[188] They also knew that if they gave up their lives for the mission, even that sacrifice would bear fruit in God's economy.

The readers of their letters heard more about the war from inside China than most Americans would have heard from the newspapers, and they had come to care about the Chinese men and women who worked for the mission or whose stories were being told. One subscriber wrote to say that he loved *Kinamissionæren*, especially the letters from the missionaries and wished there could be many more. Through them he learned the situation of the missionaries in their work and play. "Often," he wrote, "tears come when I read the paper—but they are tears of joy, when I hear of something about how the word was spread, how it was spoken. I hope that in its own time this will bear fruit. The missionaries plant, and the Lord gives the growth for Jesus' sake."[189]

The Women's Work Takes Hold | 143

The rise of the women's movement, even in the churches, meant that women both at home and on the mission field were beginning to have more and more say in the workings of the church and their own work in the church. The February 2, 1895, edition of *Budbæreren* printed a remarkable letter from Mrs. Østen Hanson in answer to an editorial from Christoffer Brøhaugh, a leader of the Hauge Synod's China Mission. He had, like Herman Preus, pleaded with the women to give money, not only to the mission but also to the synod seminary. Mrs. Hanson responded with an ever so slightly arch tone, "We send money to the schools; we have done much for our schools." What was bothering the men was the money they saw going to the missionaries—especially during the difficult times during the financial panic of 1893—instead of their institutions at home which also needed support. Ever since Gustava Kielland, the leaders of the women's societies all had said: Women's first duty was in the home, then the home congregation, then foreign missions. Both in China and in the United States, the leaders of the women's societies watched closely to make sure they were observing these rules in order not to unnecessarily provoke the men in leadership.

The China Mission Society's work in China was growing at a faster clip than their small numbers could support, but they confidently set out with the building of even more centers. In January, Netland announced that they had opened another station in Fancheng where he and his wife were now working alone, giving medical attention to whomever needed it. All were praying for a doctor to come. With thanksgiving, the society heard that a Miss Ragnhild Botner (1868-1955) was studying in New York to be a doctor and had felt the call to be a medical missionary in China. She had come to visit relatives in Faribault for her summer vacation and even had spoken to a mission festival about the work into which she was being called. The editors urged the society to support her with prayer and gifts. Given their need for such a person, she seemed to be an answer to prayer. After one more year of school, she would be able to serve as a medical missionary in China, which was exactly what they had been praying to happen. It filled them with thanksgiving to know their prayers were being answered.[190]

Li Hongzhang, the man known as China's Bismark, was quoted as saying if Christianity were to find its way into the Chinese heart, it would be the doctors who would have opened the doors for it to come in. It was widely understood among the Chinese that almost every mission station had its own Christian doctor. As Netland and Halvor had noted, the medical workers had been path breakers for the faith there.[191]

Ragnhild Botner

The girls' school in Fancheng was being taught by the two unmarried women, Olava and Thea. By the new year of 1895, they had forty girls enrolled in the school. It was difficult at first because of how foreign it was to the Chinese to educate girls. At the same time, they knew that a Chinese woman who could teach the girls would have been most attractive to the families who sent their girls to the school. It was, however, impossible to find a Chinese woman teacher since it went against Chinese tradition to educate women. Stories about the treatment of little girls in China continued to be front and center in the magazine, because they clearly showed the problem and most surely raised funds for the mission. Oppegaard reprinted a letter from the Norwegian missionary, Gertine Johnsen, about a little boy who brought his mother to them for treatment. She was clearly depressed, if not out of her mind. She could not sleep, could not work, or do anything of use. When they began talking to her, they were horrified to hear that she had killed her lovely eight-year-old daughter by tying a stone around her and, with the help of her husband, throwing her into the river.[192] This story raised great concern among their supporters at home and brought them small gifts from around the church.

The Netlands had moved into a house in the middle of Fancheng—a fine building, 280 feet long and thirty-six feet wide. In it they would have a girls' and a boys' school, and place for a church or chapel. It had taken a great deal of haggling with both the owner and the mandarin to get the deal closed. And, as in the previous deliberations for the first house, just when they thought they were done, it had only just begun. They were continuing to learn how important it was for the Chinese to be able to save face.[193]

Knowing this made the process go somewhat quicker. By May 4, 1895, there were twenty-three students enrolled in the school. Most frustrating to the women was their command of the language. As Oline wrote, "When we speak the way we have learned in the books, the people understand very little of what we have said, which is very trying."[194]

The women at home were busy not only gathering their nickels for the mission, but also sending things they had made by hand. Thea thanked a Hauge Synod women's group for sending a blanket to the mission. In her comments she seemed still overcome with the conditions in China, both politically and in their smaller world. She could still not get over the difference between her world and theirs. "There is in most houses a urine smell. Sickness surely comes as a result of the urine. When the Chinese women visit us, they are shocked at our clean floors."[195] The Netlands' most pressing work continued to be their medical work. They knew as the summer heat began, the number of sick would increase, which would make their work much harder and more difficult.

The ubiquitous Nestegaards still were coming and going from the China mission among the Norwegians and Norwegian-Americans as they also tried to establish work in Mongolia. The May 1895 issue of *Budbæreren* had a note from the editor, Østby, stating that Halvor had reported the elder Nestegaard had received a bad report from several missionaries including the China Inland Mission and Hudson Taylor. Editor Østby asked, "When will friends of the mission here at home learn to know this man for what he is?"[196] Whether Østby had any actual facts about the man is not clear, but it is of interest to note that the book by and about the Nestegaards was published that same year, about that time.[197]

On January 18, 1895, Thea wrote a long letter home, now to *Budbæreren*, partly in response to the split that was occurring between the Hauge Synod and the China Mission Society, which pained her. "We did not like the report on the society's last meeting and have not heard what the Hauge Synod did, but we will remain Haugians."[198] From then on her letters appear in *Budbæreren*, not *Kinamissionaren*, given that they had decided with which organization they would work, and she had chosen along with her brother to stay with the Hauge Synod. She concludes her letter with a description of the school:

> I have been stronger this winter than before. It is very

difficult to be sick and study this difficult language. We have forty girls in our girls' school. It was late that we got the school and few girls came. We couldn't find a woman teacher, since that goes against Chinese custom. . . . One cent a day buys coals for their feet which hurt because they are so ruined. They often sit and hold them up and weep. Poor children! They believe they should do so and set great honor upon having the smallest feet. When we talk to the parents about this, they say it is our custom and we cannot overthrow it. When will the Chinese wake up and see how bad this is? Now we have started to make house calls and then we really discover need. We talk to the women and children about God. It is so new they cannot fathom it, but God's Spirit has power and can open the heathen heart.[199]

The binding of little girls' feet was difficult for the missionaries to confront because it had been deeply engrained in Chinese culture for nearly a thousand years. It had begun among the nobility, perhaps as a way to show they were rich that the women did not need to work—rather like the practice of growing one's fingernails to extreme lengths, which showed that the one with the long fingernails never engaged in manual labor. Making the woman's feet small by breaking the arch bones and lifting them up against the ankle gave the women a kind of swaying gait that Chinese men were said to have found to be sexually alluring. The process took years and subjected the little girls to untold agony. It meant watching so that the toenails did not infect the whole foot. Frequently the toes did get infected, and they dropped off. Sometimes the process caused the little girl to die of gangrene poisoning. It is not difficult to understand the horror Americans felt at the process, but when they arrived they were somewhat baffled by what to do to change a thousand-year

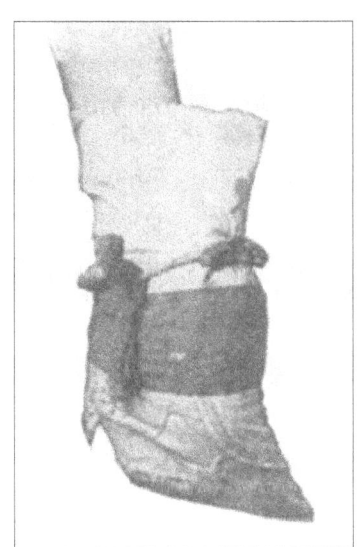
Bound foot

custom. While the practice was said to involve almost all the girls among the upper classes, it was followed somewhat less among the poor, especially the farmers, who needed their daughters to help them in the fields. Many of the rulers of China issued edicts against the practice, but the Chinese feared that if they did not bind their daughters' feet, they would never marry and would remain a burden to their families. It was not practiced much among the Manchu of the north, so the dynasty did not recommend it, but it was still deeply engrained among many in the area where the Norwegian-Americans were. A society called Heavenly Feet banned the practice among its followers, but it was finally banned when the Qing dynasty collapsed in 1911-1912 under the democratic revolution initiated by Sun Yatsen. There are reportedly some Chinese women who still bear the scars of the practice with a pronounced limp, but their numbers are few today.[200] At that time women, who suffered from this process as well as the entire hierarchical system, were a fallow field for the gospel. The Chinese culture's attitude toward women, with its system of child brides, often meant delivering the young girl over to bondage in her husband's family. This would mean being ruled over by the mother-in-law who now finally had power. She frequently caused the kind of suffering she had experienced in her own journey through the system.

It was no wonder the women missionaries worked to establish girls' schools almost as soon as they could speak the language. Olava Hodnefield described the school and the work in which both she and Thea were involved. Sometimes it was frustrating work: When they went to women to "tell them about their immortal souls, they want to know what we wear and how we live."[201] Olava noted what many other women missionaries had said about Chinese women: Their needs were so dire and their lives so impoverished that they could only concentrate on what was before them and could rarely think of things beyond what was happening to them at the moment. Lottie Moon, the famous Southern Baptist missionary, had written some years before that Chinese women were so abused they were surprised to see anyone pay any attention to them. When the missionary tried to point beyond herself to Jesus, they would smile dumbly and look uncomprehendingly at her, remarking that the missionaries would care for them. Thea said much the same thing in a later letter. "The women are so different from us. They don't think about anything but what they see before their eyes."[202] In the middle of the story of Jesus, women would interrupt the missionary and ask the most prosaic questions about life in America. One woman is said to have asked a missionary whether or not her husband beat her, drank too much or otherwise abused her. When the missionary said, no, the Chinese woman would sigh that she had no business talking of a place like heaven for women after they died. It was apparent that the American women were living in heaven right then.[203] Such accounts stirred the readers to further effort. Many readers wrote to offer money to buy a slave girl whose fate grieved the Rønnings. Countless others wrote to say they were sending money to respond to one or another of the needs demonstrated by the missionary letters. Apparently letters from the girls in the Mission Bands were a surprise to the editor, Christian Brøhaugh, who encouraged women to write to *Budbæreren*. "This is your paper, too," he said. "We'll fix up the errors if we have to."[204]

Christian Brøhaugh

HEAT, ILLNESS, AND DANGER

In a letter to *Børnevennen*, (*The Children's Friend*) the magazine for children in the Hauge Synod later edited by her brother Nils, Thea thanked the children for sending the song book, *Harpelegeren med guitarskole* in which there was a self-teaching book on how to play the guitar, something she had planned to learn, but had not found the time. Writing in April, she was dreading the coming of the hot summer. "Summer is lovely in China," she said. "It is lovely in the field, but awful in the houses." She then told a story which her readers would never forget. The group had been invited to the home of some people they knew, and when they got in they saw a casket. "I thought it was empty, but when I smelled the terrible smell I said, 'Is there anyone in that casket?' Yes, my husband's father" was the answer.[205] Then she regretted how little she could actually do as she walked around the station. "All must eat pain (*spise smerte*—a common saying in Chinese) in China!" One thing that bothered her a bit was that their school was less visited than it had been. This was very likely caused by the growing antipathy to foreigners that had endangered many missionaries that year and would result in a brutal slaughter of ten English missionaries north of them.

Another conflict that had simmered among friends of the mission was the one between O. S. Nestegaard the elder and officials in almost all mission societies. From the restlessness of his travels and inability to stay in one place for any time, it appears he may have had some kind of mental problem or attention deficit disorder. He clearly had trouble convincing the leadership of China Inland Mission, the Hauge Synod, or any number of groups that he could be trusted. His main difficulty at this time was his conflict with Østby, the editor and treasurer of the China Mission Society. For some reason, Nestegaard had offended Østby. In their meeting in South Friborg congregation in Ottertail County, Minnesota, the society was debating whether or not to send Nestegaard as their missionary. Apparently Østby had written offensive accusations against Nestegaard.²⁰⁶ When the Hauge Synod had refused to call him because he was un-Lutheran, he had gone to the professors at Augsburg Seminary. The faculty there had found him to be Lutheran and, with that recommendation, he returned again to the Hauge Synod leaders. After lengthy meetings with the council and an official apology from both Østby and Nestegaard, they were reconciled. According to the report from Hans Arneson Gaardsmoe (1857-1923), secretary of the organization, after the apologies were heard, they shook hands, tears running down their faces. One of the pastors there, Jørgen Danielson Swalestuen (1867-1946), wrote that he had never been to such a meeting that had resulted in such a blessed compromise, something he could never forget. "We have experienced that God has been with us, and that he has heard the many prayers sent to him in this case, wherefore we now should give thanks to God."²⁰⁷ This relationship however would once again be changed with new reports from China (see Appendix 1).

On April 18, 1895, the Treaty of Shimonoseki declaring peace between China and Japan was signed. In the war and in the treaty China had lost its hegemony over Korea and had to recognize its independence. In addition it ceded the Pescadores and Formosa to Japan. Finally, it had to open four more ports to commerce with Japan and the West. Although the war was over officially, the defeat had brought shame to China and antagonized the Chinese, both mandarin and peasant, against any foreign devils, so the missionaries felt themselves to be under growing threat, despite their good relations with the people in Fancheng. That summer of 1895 the heat, although it cannot be said to be the cause of the illnesses that plagued them, certainly made it much more difficult to get well. Halvor had been so sick with malaria from April through early summer that he nearly died. He wrote that he was so weak that he could barely walk. When he became well enough to stand, he had to learn to walk again almost like a little child. Just when he thought he was improving and was able to write the letter, his fever began to climb again, and Hannah added a note that he was worse.²⁰⁸ Hannah had also been ill for several days, as had Miss Hodnefield, who traveled to Laohoutian to seek treatment from an English doctor, but had not improved. Thea wrote on May 19 that Halvor was better, as were the two children, Nilius and Kjerstin, now learning to sing and wanting to sing the old Norwegian folk song, "*Paal sine høne*," to Thea's amusement. They had taught them about their grandparents and aunts and uncles in Norway so they could speak of them as though they knew them. She also commented on Halvor's weakness and inability to walk, so bad they had feared it was rheumatic fever, but they decided it was not that, even though he was still just barely able to walk.[209]

Miss Hodnefield continued to suffer from her illness and needed further treatment, so she and the Netlands tried to escape the heat and went to Hankow on June 20 where she could be treated by Dr. Helgeson of the Norwegian mission. This had helped her to recover some of her strength, although the heat was so oppressive that she could barely write the note informing the mission concerning her health.[210] Rest was what she needed and relief from the heat. In an added page to this letter Thea noted that she too was sick again, partly because of the heat. She did allow that being ill had its good side for in that trial "one had to ask are all my sins forgiven, and am I washed in the blood of the Lamb?"[211]

The Netlands, exhausted from the requirements of the jobs they—and especially he—had, nearly non-stop work in the clinic they had established, traveled to Shanghai and then Nagasaki, Japan, for a rest, away from the terrible heat and the filth of China. The missionaries noted that Japan, for some reason, had always been much cleaner than China. Drinking clean fresh water from a spring by their little cabin was like a miracle to him after his time in China. They returned on August 10, where they heard for the first time of the ten English missionaries who had been killed most savagely on August 4 in Huashan, near Gucheng, in northern China. Despite the dangers, they left quickly for Fancheng and their work, a long and tedious journey by boat up the Han River. In his report to the China Mission Society, Netland spoke highly of the work Thea and Olava had been able to do with women: "Since there are women here at the station, there are many Chinese women who come to the meetings. That is as it should be, and it fills us with joy."[212]

Thea wrote home from Fancheng on August 19, regretting the long time since she had written. The floods of the Han River, historic in this year, had taken many homes and many lives. She wanted to report that their situation was safe, although they may have heard of the uprising in North China where missionaries and their stations had been attacked, but none killed. The worst was in southern China where missionaries had been killed and several wounded. She expressed her confidence that the Lord was in charge. She did, however, give her parents an accounting of those killed: Three were children, eight were women, and one man had been killed. Her family, however, was not to worry. It was not as dangerous where they were as it was in northern China where the war was being fought. One report, however, from Sophie Clausen seems from this distance to portend doom. After describing the death of the English missionaries, she added, "There appears to be a secret organization over all of China. Without a doubt they want to kill all foreigners."[213] With the perfect vision of hindsight, one hears in this off comment the rising of the Boxer movement which would culminate in the siege of those in the foreign legations during the summer of the Boxer Rebellion's most violent period in 1900.

The summer of 1895 had been fairly cool, with probably too much rain, in contrast to the year before when it had been warmer than it had ever been. What troubled Thea most was that they had found a little girl baby thrown out on the river bank, face down in the sand. They thought it was about one or two months old. For Thea it was a sign of a gruesome culture that could throw away babies, especially girl babies, partly because of poverty, but also because a girl's life was not worth as much as a little boy. Chinese parents were learning they could leave babies with the missionaries and they would thrive, although the missionaries had to be very careful not to buy the children nor take them in too freely because of the rumor often bruited about that the missionaries bought children to misuse them.[214] Later Olava Hodnefield would write to *Børnevennen* about this incident:

> Such a sweet little baby, left alone to die on the river bank, had not Christians found her. She was carried to the house by the doorkeeper. Mrs. Rønning took and washed and dressed her. I wish you could have seen her as she was lying in her arms. So innocently did she look up into Mrs. Rønning's eyes, as if to say, "Will you care for me now since my mother has left me?"[215]

THEA MEETS LANDAHL

In November of 1895 Thea returned to Hankow from Fancheng in order to meet some new missionaries who had just come from the Hauge Synod, especially Pastor Thorstein Himle and his family. Carl Landahl (Carl W. Carlson, 1870-1964) was also traveling with the Himles, and he intended to work with the Rønnings in Fancheng. Thea had left Fancheng for Hankow on October 14 and had traveled for two weeks before she arrived. She wrote her family in Norway from Hankow, October 28, explaining that she had gone to meet the new arrivals because they needed someone who could speak Chinese well enough to bring them to the inland, since none of them spoke Chinese. Reporting on life back at the missionary compound in Fancheng, she noted that the house was not as healthy a place as it could have been, making it difficult for Nilius, Halvor and Hannah's oldest son, to thrive. He was plagued by constant fevers and generally had a weak constitution. From there she moved, as usual, to things spiritual. It was also a grief to her that those at home in Norway were also dealing with issues of poor health, especially her mother. Although illnesses and epidemics were much more common in China than Norway, partly because of the large populations living in such close quarters without any sanitation, it is important to remember that common diseases still took their toll among people everywhere. God's hand in the preservation of good health

Carl Landahl

was clear to them. It was God who gave and took away, using many means, even among those who loved him, to bring about good.[216] Thinking that they would not receive the letter until Christmas she included Christmas greetings thinking of their far-flung family—Nils in America, their parents in Norway, and them in China. No matter where they were, she rejoiced that they could all stand around the Christ child who was with them.[217]

The separation of the Hauge Synod from the China Mission Society had caused some hard feelings in the States, but the missionaries in China did not feel those rifts between them and their colleagues in China; they needed each other too much. *Budbæreren*, the official organ of the Hauge Synod, had created a *Kinamission* section in which news of the mission and the letters of Thea and her brother were published, as well as the *Children's Friend*, a magazine for children which would later be edited by her brother, Nils N. Rønning. In that paper, the children of the Hauge Synod could read the letters from the missionaries written especially to them. Those letters made it possible for the young people to follow the work of the missionaries. It was one of the reasons the children of the Hauge Synod came to feel quite strongly for the missionaries and their Chinese helpers. Many of those readers would write in to say they had given their hearts to Jesus and were certain he was calling them to be missionaries to China. Certainly these brave women gave the young children growing up in the Hauge Synod a sense of vocational choice and adventure that must have made a profound difference in their later lives.

In the letters we can see, as well, how Thea was gaining mastery of Chinese culture and the language. On October 12, 1895, Halvor wrote to *Budbæreren* saying that Thea was going to Hankow to meet the Himles and Landahl and bring them to Fancheng because without knowing Chinese they could not be expected to travel on their own.[218] That Thea was chosen to do this shows that she had become rather competent in Chinese and in her own confidence. On November 11, 1895, Thea wrote to *Børnevennen* from Hankow, telling of her trip down the river and what she found when she got there. Unfortunately, the Himles, who had traveled with Landahl from America, had not made it to Hankow. Their two oldest children were hospitalized in Shanghai with diphtheria and scarlet fever. After they recovered, Mrs. Himle had to be hospitalized for what her husband called nerve fever. Because the letter from Thea was both public and a letter to her brother Nils, the editor of the children's magazine, she also informed him about the health of the family back in Fancheng: Little Nilius and Sigfrid Netland were both ill with whooping cough.

The trip to Hankow, which usually took some days, had done her good. The change of air for her as well as a change in her daily routine made it possible for her to rest while the boat made its way down the river. By this time, her life had become somewhat routine, if not monotonous, with the daily lessons in Chinese along with her work with the women, either at home or in the school, or on visits. Despite this routine, however, she took joy in it because it gave her peace, something she needed in the face of the great burden of getting the gospel out to the Chinese so they could be converted to the living God. All things are possible for God, she concluded, with her usual request, "Pray for us!"[219]

Gidske Himle

None of the letters Thea sent from Hankow mentioned that she was also going to meet Landahl. Her main concern had been the Himles whose health situation was growing worse by the day with the two younger children now sick unto death with smallpox. She and the Daniel Nelsons had gone to meet the boats from Shanghai several times a day, but neither Landahl nor the Himles arrived. When Landahl did arrive in Hankow, he was not expecting to be greeted at the pier because he had not been able to inform them of his arrival. To his surprise, he spotted Thea and Nelson in the crowd and, after a joyful greeting, they took him home where he could stay and rest. When they arrived at the Nelsons, they broke into a song of thanksgiving to the living God and then read Psalm 23, with the verse, "Thou hast prepared a table before me in the presence of mine enemies." He had further information on Mrs. Gidske Himle who was ill with something called nerve fever, a result of typhus which caused vertigo and other debilitating symptoms. The course of the disease was around two or three weeks, but it left the patient extremely weak. Just as she was recovering her strength and they were preparing to travel to Hankow, the two youngest children died of smallpox. After their funerals, Mrs. Himle collapsed again and had to return to the hospital where she had to stay for a long time to recover her strength. Even after her illness had left her, she was still so weak that she had to be carried up and down stairs.

Thea and Landahl, along with another Swedish missionary, left for Fancheng, a 400 mile journey.[220] Landahl wrote as they were leaving, regretting that the Himles, with whom he had traveled to China and whom he had gotten to know well, had to stay in Shanghai until she recovered from her illness. Landahl and Thea hoped to arrive in Fancheng by Christmas so they could celebrate the holiday with the missionaries gathered there. It is interesting to read their letters as their relationship develops. We as readers know they will marry. He probably knew Thea from his acquaintance with Halvor

Red Wing Seminary in Red Wing, Minnesota.

and had very likely heard her speaking during the many farewell parties around Faribault and Red Wing where he was studying as they prepared to leave. Thus he recognized her at the pier in Hankow, but there is no hint of a romantic relationship of any kind in the letters, although they generally reveal very little of such things.

Thea Meets Landahl | 157

On the long trip, usually a month, the three missionaries had the leisure to get to know each other well, and it was probably the beginning or the continuation of the romance between Landahl and Thea. It probably would have been a bit strange for her to go to Hankow if there had not been some previous relationship between them. On the other hand, for two single missionaries of the opposite sex to be together so long, without chaperones, is rather surprising since Halvor and Hannah had married immediately upon arriving in China to avoid any whisper of a scandal.

Carl W. Landahl had come to the United States in October 1888 from Sweden to work with his brother, who had emigrated earlier and had a farm near Dexter, Minnesota, a small town near Albert Lea. He had heard about the China mission from Halvor, who served the Dexter congregation for a brief period before leaving for China. He had spoken to the congregation in Dexter about the China mission at a Christmas service, according to Landahl, who remembered it well. When he heard Rønning, he felt called to attend Red Wing Seminary so he could prepare to be a missionary in China. He enrolled at the seminary in 1891, the fall that Thea and Halvor left for China. Landahl completed his degree in 1895 and was ordained that summer, leaving for China in the fall of the year. Almost immediately upon his arrival he began writing lengthy letters home which show him to be a careful observer of the life around him.

While Thea was gone, Halvor had finally got permission to begin building the mission station in Fancheng. His frustrations with the Chinese laws and regulations after two years of failure had reached a fever pitch. He included in his letter home documents from the American consul in Hankow, Charles Denby. On September 23, the missionaries received a note from Beijing: "Have instructed consul Hankow to demand viceroy to issue orders to magistrate that you have right under Berthemy Convention to purchase land without prior authorization of officials. Insist on right, demand Yamen to issue same orders. Denby."[221] Halvor's joy at having the issue resolved set him to building immediately, almost as though he feared the magistrate would return and change his mind. At the end of his letter describing the situation with the building, he added a postscript: "Thea and Brother Landahl had left Hankow with the

Swedish missionary Sjøquist November 26, and they are expected any day." It was rather late in the year for such a trip to be comfortable in the Chinese junks that brought passengers up and down the river, and Halvor worried that the freezing weather would make it an uncomfortable trip for the three. In addition they had heard that several Swedish missionaries had been set upon by robbers and lost all of their luggage.[222]

Before they left Hankow, Thea had written Martin G. Hanson, vice president of the Hauge Synod and an active member of the China Mission Society of the Hauge Synod, describing the situation as she waited for the Himles and Landahl. She had known the Himles back in Faribault and had awaited their arrival eagerly. When Landahl finally arrived in Hankow on November 13, he brought greetings to Thea from their friends at home. Because they wanted to get back to Fancheng before Christmas, they left on November 26, before the worst of the winter weather made their trip uncomfortable. One of the reasons she probably was longing to be with her family on Christmas was that she had just heard that her mother had died. Being with Halvor would be a comfort to her, even if they were certain that their mother was at home with God.[223]

Landahl had enjoyed being in Shanghai where, despite his sorrow over the illnesses of the much besieged Himles, he had been able to tour Shanghai with his newly found friend, John Waitlow, a Danish missionary on his way to Nüchuang. Together they saw the sights and attended a meeting at St. John's College, which had been built to educate native Chinese who wanted to be teachers and evangelists of the faith. Established in 1879 by the Anglicans, it was the most prestigious school in China at the time, educating many Chinese leaders of the day. The topic of the meeting, which had attracted seventy-five women and men missionaries, had been a pressing one for the missionaries: whether or not to send Chinese students to boarding schools. The result of their deliberations was that they should send students there since boarding schools were the hotbeds for cultivating future pastors and evangelists for China. That had been an interesting time for Carl because he could meet many other missionaries devoted to their common task. Furthermore, because he was staying at the Missionary Home of the China Inland Mission headquarters, he had the privilege of meeting Hudson Taylor. To see the old man and hear him welcome them to the great mission field of China thrilled Landahl. "It was moving," he said, "to see the old giant, who is now truly old and filled with his days after such a long time of work."[224]

Hudson Taylor

Taylor, although still an active man, was now harvesting the results of his years of work. Missionaries were pouring into China from Europe and America. From 1891 to 1896 over a thousand missionaries had come to China—672 women and 481 men. The imbalance of women over men shows how women especially had heard the cries of the Chinese women and answered out of Christian love with their own lives, along with not a little spirit of adventure.[225] No doubt it was also a place where they could exercise their own Christian vocations in a more forward way than at home, since there were few executives around forbidding them their call to preach or otherwise minister to a congregation. *The Lutheran* (*Lutheraneren*), now the organ of the United Church, was edited by Carl Otto Aubol (1860-1939), who was originally from the Norwegian Synod, but who now had moved from the Anti-Missourian Brotherhood to be a leader of the United Church. He was reporting on these facts, sharing that the China Mission Society and the Hauge Synod's support for the mission in China had wider support than from their own kind. Many such reports would appear in its pages, which only increased the interest in the China mission. The usual complaints against the women for gathering simply to gossip or raise money through bazaars or dinners always thrummed beneath the genuine admiration of the editors. A note in the December 12, 1895, issue of *The Lutheran* rejoiced that some women's groups were now getting together to raise money without bazaars![226] They reported on the idea of a Cent Society, in which women, girls, and Luther Leagues could gather pennies that they would set into little books especially made to hold usually 100 pennies. It had been done by American Protestant missionary societies for many years, as well as in Norway, with the *Ørebøger*, books for collecting *øre*, the smallest Norwegian coin.

A nickel society had transformed the Presbyterian women's mission ingathering and caused the male leadership great concern that the women should have gathered in so much money over which they had no control. Many meetings and many resolutions were discussed and passed with little effect, because the male leadership wanted the money for its own dispensing. One thing is clear: The leaders of the various churches were well aware that it was the women who would raise the most money. One might describe their hearts as divided on this issue, because at the same time that they knew the women would generously support missions with successful drives for money, they also coveted it for their own institutions, especially their schools which never had enough money and for which they were constantly raising funds. One sees this clearly articulated in an article in *The Lutheran* on what women's and girl's organizations could do. The conclusion was straightforward: raise a lot of money![227]

The Landahl party arrived in Fancheng the week before Christmas. Hannah wrote that Landahl brought with him news of their good friends back in Minnesota and Iowa. His coming with that news, she commented, was a refreshing break in their life in the mission station. "It was a great joy for us to meet him, a refreshing change in our monotonous life." Not only had he brought greetings from home, "but gifts from our loved ones. Mixed feelings moved around in our inner selves. In such an occasion, more than in others, we realize that we are a long way from relatives and friends." The women by this time were using the term "monotonous" (*ensformige Liv*) to describe their lives several times in this patch of letters home. They never explained it other than to suggest that they were confined to a small world and could not leave without some protection, and they had now lived together for some time in the same quarters. It also shows that they seemed to have fallen into a very strict routine of studying the language, working with the women and children in their care, in addition to their own many housekeeping duties in the compound. Quite naturally, news from home and visitors was awaited eagerly. Their one concern at the writing of this letter on January 14, 1896, was the health of the Himles and Mrs. Himle's illness which had kept them in Shanghai.

Hannah described the recent Christmas celebrations as having been peaceful. If only the Chinese would see their need for a Savior,

First congregational meeting in Taipingdian

she sighed! While it was calm in their city at the time, there had just been an incident in their neighborhood when over fifty thieves had plundered and stolen all that was in the homes of some neighbors. What could you expect, she concluded, when they are all so poor?[228] As 1896 began, Halvor continued his carpentry work on the building in Fancheng, now ably assisted by Landahl, whose letters home from the mission station in Fancheng were a mixture of homily and news of the missionaries. Now that he was safely settled in the station, he was both studying the language and observing the new world into which he had come. The news from the Himles kept getting worse. Now they had heard about the death of the two youngest of the Himles, and their sorrow was almost unbearable. Since Landahl had traveled with the family on the long trip from America to Shanghai, he was especially grieved about the deaths of the young children. He made an effort to understand the reason that God would put these fine people to such a test. He mused on the question one often asked: Who had sinned, they or their parents? That was not the right question, he concluded. Maybe they were like Job, righteous and faithful, whom God loved. His troubles did not come from his sin, but as a test and trying that cleansed him. He could not say, only that they would one day understand. God was still the author of all things, and God's ways were not ours. He concluded that they had heard from the Himles that Gidske was finally improving, but that Himle was sunk in grief and sorrow. "No wonder. Let us pray for them," he exclaimed.²²⁹ The stories of the death of the little Himle children were so searing that one woman in Duluth sent *Børnevennen* five dollars to buy a tombstone for them in their resting place in Shanghai.²³⁰ In a postscript to the last letter that could be sent before everything stopped for the Chinese New Year celebrations, Landahl described the river bank in front of the station from which they could see over 100 boats. While we have no picture of this scenic outlook, we do know that the area with its river and surrounding mountains looked to them a lot like the fjords at home in Norway. Later Edwin Himle, who was with the Landahls while his parents went to Shanghai, had Landahl write to his parents, "Here it is lovely—a large house with many trees."

Hannah Rorem Rønning

Late that winter, Hannah and Thea again began hosting meetings with the women and children in the house, which had stopped while they were moving from the old house to their new one, Landahl wrote.²³¹ As they were trying to build up their mission, they realized that their region of China was beginning to suffer a great drought, which would turn out to be one of the worst in recorded history. The missionaries feared, with good reason, they would be pointed to as the cause of the drought. Landahl, now much engaged in the building of the mission with Rønning, wrote home to say that at first in a drought the Chinese would pray to their gods and try to please them. When that failed, however, they would begin blaming the missionaries for bringing an unknown god to them and angering their gods. Then the lives of the missionaries would be in danger.²³² Ultimately, the historians agree that the drought of 1896 resulted in unrest among the people, with their lives becoming worse and worse, until the Boxer Rebellion boiled over in 1900. Landahl described a trip outside of the city, where he saw the dry fields and the people burning paper to their gods, and a widow with five children who wanted to give at least one to the missionaries. Although they would have liked to have taken the child in, it would ultimately be a bad decision. Not only would thousands of others want to do the same, the rumor would spread wildly that the missionaries used the children's bodies for medicine. All they could do was provide food for the widow so she could feed her children.[233]

Since the missionaries were under frequent suspicion, violence against them was not uncommon. Netland complained that the Chinese regime was not able to protect foreigners and was impossible to work with.[234] Although the missionaries wrote frequently to say they were not in danger, missionaries in their region were being attacked and killed. It is fairly clear that these young people were able to make good friends with their neighbors and, although they had some rather frightening experiences, they never felt themselves to be in mortal danger.

By the first of May, when the river was at its height from the spring runoff, the Himles were about to arrive in Fancheng accompanied by Halvor Rønning, who had gone to Hankow to help them on their way. Landahl was eager to meet them, so he rented a small boat and began traveling toward where he supposed he might find them. All of a sudden, he heard voices crying to him that there were Americans coming. Then he heard the voice of the young boy, Edwin Himle, "Here comes Landahl!" They lifted him up into their boat, and he was surprised to see that Mrs. Himle looked well, as did Himle and Edwin. Very shortly after they landed. Landahl went ahead to the station where he found thieves taking things from their belongings.[235] He got rid of the thieves. The Himles arrived, and in the morning they, the Rønnings, and Landahl celebrated their reunion after many long months.

The heat of the Chinese summer would soon overtake the young missionary families. Nothing was so debilitating to them as the heat. They wrote only those letters that seemed absolutely necessary. They did, however, feel it important to report home on the Himle's arrival. Mrs. Himle marveled that it was a miracle she had survived her illness in Shanghai, something she noted was probably because her hour glass had not yet run out. Being sick in the heat of the Chinese summer was not easy, she concluded.[236] Despite the searing heat, even in August 1896, Thea appeared to be the healthiest she had ever been. She had been helping with the children at the station, serving as aunt to all, especially her brother's children since Hannah had contracted a case of smallpox despite having been vaccinated, as they all had. She had apparently caught it from the patients who had come to Himle's office, which was in the room next to the Rønning's bedroom.[237]

After Himle arrived, Thea had new purpose: Now she could help him with his medical work by translating for the women patients. Before he had come to China, the Hauge Synod had sent him to a short medical course at the University of Minnesota so that he would be able to give medical help when he arrived. Now that he was working, it was apparent to all that they needed a larger facility for their clinic, maybe even a hospital with rooms where patients who had endured a long trip to their clinic could stay overnight.

ENGAGEMENT, NEAR DEATH, MARRIAGE, AND HONEYMOON

It was during this time that Landahl asked Thea to marry him. Thea does not mention it in her letters to the church paper, but there is an intriguing loose page of a letter in the family's private collection in which she describes Landahl to her family. They will receive a picture of him soon, she said. He was not quite Halvor's height, has dark hair, dark blue eyes, and was rather handsome. That, however, she was quick to say, was not why she was marrying him—almost as though such considerations were unworthy. They are bound in their love for Jesus Christ. For that reason she was asking them to pray that they will receive the blessings of God and also the blessings of her father and siblings. They had a great work to do and needed the prayers of everyone. Of that she was certain.[238]

Although Thea's health had never been better, that summer was particularly trying to the missionaries. It was exceedingly hot, and cholera raged through Hankow and other northern cities. Thea and Olava were out making house calls in Fancheng almost through July, surely exposing themselves to the disease as well as other infectious diseases. On August 15, to their great shock, Netland died of cholera. Most of the missionaries attributed his death to his extreme exhaustion from the medical work he was doing as part of his mission work. Halvor commented on how quickly death came to them and how they would look around at each other and wonder who would be next. At the time Hannah and Thea were doing well, although Olava seemed to be suffering relapses from her original illness, which was never quite diagnosed.[239] Netland's widow, Oline, was also very sick with cholera, but she recovered and left China shortly thereafter with Netland's daughter and the child they had together, returning to Minnesota. There she lived and spoke about the China mission throughout the church to great effect. That fall, Thea and Landahl planned to be married, something we only know in retrospect as their colleagues report on their nearly fatal illnesses. The couple had left Fancheng for Hankow, where the Nelsons were and where Mrs. Netland had gone before sailing for America. Just after she left, Mrs. Nelson came down with cholera. Nelson had been almost certain she was going to die, and she was still very weak when Thea arrived for the wedding. Just before the marriage, Landahl was stricken with malaria and was not expected to live. According to a letter he had written on October 18, 1896, he had been ill with a hard fever for ten long weeks and near death several times. When Thea arrived for the wedding in Hankow, she found her husband-to-be too ill to talk. Under her care, he recovered, miraculously, but just as they were going to be married, Thea, who had been staying with the Nelsons, came down with cholera. Thea's case was a very bad one, Mrs. Lars Kristenson reported in a letter to *Budbæreren* in 1897. Thea, now under the care of Dr. Thompson whom the missionaries regarded as especially skilled, was given up for dead. She had been a faithful nurse to Landahl and perhaps became ill out of sheer exhaustion, something the missionaries admitted was possible. However, even when she arrived in Hankow for the wedding, she looked exhausted. As the Chinese outside the compound were dying by the hundreds, their unclaimed bodies baking in the sun, Thea struggled for life. Landahl, finally well enough to get out of bed, was told to leave the house before he, too, came down with cholera and perished. Mrs. Kristenson described Landahl's departure, which the doctor prescribed so he would not also come down with the disease. He called out to Thea that one day, in heaven, they would meet again. Then he left, thinking he would never see her in this life. Thea knew little of what was transpiring; her pain was so debilitating. She wrote later that she had felt incredibly close to God when she heard Landahl calling softly, "Farewell and God's peace until we meet again!" Mrs. Kristenson, who nursed both Thea and Mrs. Nelson, wrote a letter home describing the illness of Thea:

> Her pain and cramps were awful and she got worse and worse. Finally she prayed, "O God take me home to you; I can't bear this any longer." We thought she would not live through the night. She spent the next day praying to go home. "The world is full of pain and sin," she said, "and I am loosed from the earth. Have mercy on me."

Then Mrs. Kristenson administered morphine to her, thinking to relieve her pain, but it grew more severe. Finally Thea cried, "Is God dead that he does not hear me?" Then, suddenly, after a warm bath, she got some rest. The next morning the doctor was astonished to find her alive. She was better, he said, to their great amazement. Despite what they thought was a relapse which included some mental confusion, the doctor knew that she was on the mend.

She sent greetings to her friends back home in the letter which Mrs. Kristensen wrote, saying, "I am better. Thanks so much for your letters. I am too weak to write, but soon hope to."[240] The missionaries took time spelling each other in their effort to be at her side constantly: the Nelsons, Kristenson, and Landahl's teacher would sit beside her and weep to hear her suffering so terribly. Mrs. Kristenson remarked that Thea was one of the most lovable patients for whom she had cared. Thea frequently expressed her regret that people had to sit beside her and would weep in thanksgiving for their willingness to help her. "The next time you meet either of them," Mrs. Kristenson wrote, "regard them as people who have come back from the grave."[241]

That they both recovered was regarded by the missionaries as a miracle. It had been necessary for them to come to Hankow for the marriage since Landahl was an American citizen and needed to be married in the presence of the American consul there. On October 2, 1896, they were married and immediately went north for some rest in the boat, *Yen-Woo*,

Lars Kristenson family

to Jinjiang for their honeymoon. When they were able to return to Fancheng, they would quickly prepare to move north to Shangkow. Later they decided it would be better to build in Taipingdian because of a better climate and situation, higher up, above the lowlands where mosquitos flourished. They would be able to establish a station there because of Thea's skill with the language.[242] As usual, they were accompanied by Thea's good friend Olava, who had also been in Hankow to visit a doctor. She had taken Nilius Rønning with her to receive treatment for his undiagnosed illness as well; he had been suffering occasional fevers for some time. After resting for three weeks at the retreat house, the party left to begin their work in the new city, even if they had been warned by the doctor to rest for three months because they had both been so near death. But they were young and eager to begin a new station some miles north of Fancheng in Taipingdian.[243]

Halvor had traveled to Taipingdian to look things over before he would recommend that the Landahls move there. At first he had thought they should go to Shangkow, but the place they had thought suitable for a home was too low and close to the water, something that Halvor did not think would be good for Landahl's malaria, a disease Halvor also had contracted the year before; he would suffer the typical relapses of the disease throughout his life. Hannah marveled that both Thea and Landahl were still alive, describing her grief on being separated from Nilius, and waiting for his return with the Landahls and Miss Hodnefield. She used the pain of her loss to remember from Isaiah 43 that God loved us in the same way a mother did.[244] Half homily, half news, her letter had its intended effect. The editor of the magazine, A. O. Oppegaard, recommended this letter especially for its deep spiritual content as well as its news, like many of these letters. Beneath the recommendation to read Mrs. Rønning's letter was a piece urging the members of these Ladies Aids to give money to the hospital project in Fancheng. Only 1500 dollars would be enough to finish the building. With surprising speed, they gathered in the money. The first response to the readers from the Landahls came some weeks later. Written by Landahl, most likely, it starts with an expression that sounds more Swedish than Norwegian, speaking of our "*gode Gud,*" our good God. After the usual homily, he told of their trip from Hankow to Fancheng. Because of the prevailing winds from the west, their trip took four long weeks, during which they made friends with the crew and rested. Landahl complimented the crew for being extra kind and thoughtful toward them, something that did not always happen on these boats because of what he called the usual indolence, wickedness, and wrong common among typical boat crews. Given that the journey was long, it mattered what kind of crew worked with the boat. As they were making their way up the river, they had been wary of both floods and robbers, which were especially bad at this time because of the famine caused by the floods. Things had been going fairly well, and he had remarked on it to himself. Then early one morning at dawn, before he had gotten up, members of the crew came shrieking to him, "Mr. Landahl! Get up! Get up!" They said he had to come quickly. Two of their crew had been overwhelmed by robbers and were now held as hostages. The robbers were threatening to torture the second in command. Despite Landahl's immediate fear and nervousness, he quickly dressed and found himself on deck where he discovered that what he had been told was in fact true. The crew members were, however, stronger than the thieves, so they hit them back and overcame them, to the sounds of great alarm and fear. As he saw how violently the attack was being prosecuted, Landahl cried out, but to no avail. They continued, now using their long hair pins to continue their brutal attack, breaking the table and stools into pieces. Now the bandits were outnumbered and jumped into the water and headed for a town on the other side of the river.

Still the passengers and crew had not escaped. The robbers reconnoitered and set up a blockade to stop the missionary boat, which was very slow and could not outdistance the robbers' vessel. They waited to continue their assault on the boat. Landahl had heard that this place on the river was a dangerous one with

Chinese river boat

many robbers, but still they were shocked by the number of criminals they met. As they continued their assaults, Landahl tried to get them to be less brutal against the robbers, but to no avail. Several Chinese women sitting on the river banks began screeching out that the missionaries had taken one of their own. Then a huge fracas threatened the lives and the safety of the missionaries, who were not quite sure what was happening to them. The worst were the attacks on their Chinese helpers and servants, who had suffered the most and who were now being held hostage. This in effect kept the

Landahls, Olava, and Nilius hostage because they could not proceed without them. An older missionary traveling with them, Mr. Mattson, realized that they needed official help. Under no circumstances, he warned, should they give their tormentors any money. Finally Landahl sent a man with his passport, in Chinese, to the officials—a safe conduct pass that assured Landahl could "safely and freely pass, and in case of need give him all lawful aid and protection." It was signed by the American Consul in Hankow, Charles Denby.[245]

Only after getting the magistrates to support them and threatening to send for help from Hankow were the servants of Landahl's released so the party could continue on its way. They did receive some mercy from the bandits because the missionaries treated with their medicine some of the Chinese who had been hurt in the altercations. The scene ended with a very strange ritual to the Norwegians: At the conclusion of their deliberations, Mr. Wang, their representative, took the paper they had signed, bowed three times, sighed and looked toward heaven. When he was finished, another man came in with a chicken which they killed on the table where the paper lay and let the blood run over it. He then put the chicken in the fire along with the paper and watched the smoke rise while he mumbled over and over again, "*Bangzhu, bangzhu women,*" or "Help us, Help us." After that he lay down on the floor with his face against the floor. When he stood up, the ceremony was over. Once again they began to speak with each other. Wang told them they would soon have a delicious meal out of the chicken, which they did. The Chinese drank wine and smoked pipes. Landahl's reaction was to be seriously reminded of his call: "God help us to keep the need of these heathen deep in our heart."

> Remember that picture: here lay the man with his face hidden in his hand, crying to heaven for help, asking heaven to help him. Often I heard when they prayed for good weather or favorable winds: help us, help us! When they prayed to the spirit that lived in the boat's front end beseeching heaven for help, it caused remarkable feelings deep in our souls.[246]

Finally, their people were set free and they could continue their journey north. The incident did little for the reputation of the Chinese in Landahl's mind. What they needed was the gospel and a system of law, not men. The missionaries did greet their release with great thanksgiving and surprise. Finally, they set their boat out onto the water again and made their way slowly toward Fancheng. They would arrive there in two weeks to the warmest greetings from their relatives and friends. Thinking back on the events of their capture, all Landahl could do was give thanks for God's grace, kindness, faithfulness, patience, and love that had surrounded them on their journey.[247] What Thea thought of the entire incident we do not know.

Events such as these tended to raise up much concern on the part of the women's groups at home which the church papers were quick to report. A small note in the pages of *Budbæreren* gives a small glimpse into the relationship between the Ladies Aids, their church, and the foreign mission. From the Solør Ladies Aid came the report that the women had met for the annual mission meeting on February 8, 1897. After devotions by the president, the group talked for a long time; after serious discussion and consideration, they decided to give their support to the Hauge Synod's China Mission. While nothing is said, everyone who was reading the announcement was keenly aware of the nature of the discussion. Members of that congregation remembered their pastor and his sister, and their association with the China Mission Society. It was almost certain they had loyalties not only to the Rønnings but also to the society. That they chose, finally, to support the Hauge Synod is of some interest. They would still be supporting their pastor and his sister, but they would also have to cut their ties with the society with which they had forged bonds of affection and fervor. For that reason the short announcement states that they stretched out their hands in brotherly love and went forward given the urgency of the call to do mission while it was day, before the night would come. [248]

Landahl took up his pen again, after their extreme illnesses and wedding, to report on the health of his "dear wife" (*kjere Hustru*) who was now much better. The readers of *Budbæreren* were the ones he wanted to hear first about this because he knew they had most closely followed the progress of the missionaries in China, since they knew them well and they had come from their own midst. In the same letter he told of how they were planning to extend their mission thirty miles north of Fancheng into Taipingdian which was teeming with people who needed to hear the good news. The trip to scout out the new field had gone very well; in fact,

Landahl said he felt as safe on the trip as he might have in America, although there had been an uproar on the other side of the river which concerned the relation between them and the Catholics. The rumor was that the Catholic priests had killed some Chinese, a rumor Landahl appeared to believe. While the Protestant missionaries could find agreement in their mission and gospel, most of the Protestants in China, like most Protestants at the time, found it difficult to reconcile their faith with the Catholic faith and, in fact, would preach against it to the Chinese, who would be somewhat confused by these two Western faiths being preached. How they were different was not always clear, except in their rituals.[249]

At this time, as revolution continued to roil throughout China, the missionaries who felt conditions could not be worse, took heart when they heard that the nephew of the Empress Dowager, Guangko, was reported to be in deep study of the New Testament. Furthermore, they were encouraged by the news that Li Hongzhang, China's Bismark, had named two Chinese Christian women to be delegates to the International Woman's Congress of 1898. That seemed like a good omen to them—in fact, almost unbelievable. It also showed that the Chinese regime was also casting about for something, given the chaos swirling about the entire nation. The supporters of the mission were astonished to read in *Budbæreren* that a Chinese man preaching at a New Year's festival to other Chinese had said, "Now that I have been a Christian for four or five years, I have things to say: The teachers are good people and God has given them to us. They are good to the sick and help the poor. The mandarins are not good to them, and they should be because they are helping China."[250]

Johan Skordal

Death once again visited the missionaries, this time Johan Skordal of the Norwegian mission. Halvor wrote in grief and suppressed rage back to the synod regretting the great number of missionaries who had died in service. He thought it was partly a result of the cheap way they had been forced to live. "It's stupid to spend years teaching and learning this difficult language and then having the missionaries land in the grave. It is your Christian duty to support us better!" he

Engagement, Near Death... | 173

concluded.[251] In what may have been a response to that, *Kinamissionæren* published an article on how China could not be changed without more women missionaries who could do the most effective work in China. The numbers, however, were overwhelming. Even if the Christian churches sent 100,000 missionaries, that would still mean each would have to teach over 1800 students in China, an almost hopeless challenge.[252]

Some missionaries became a bit worried about the terrible pictures they were giving their readers about China. Miss Sophie Clausen from the Norwegian mission in Laohekou, who seems to have been the most studious about things Chinese, wanted people to know how old a civilization China was and how influenced it was by Confucian thought. At its best it did have a strong moral teaching in it. Its language was very sophisticated and beautiful, but when it came to girls and women the teachings were useless. She then went on to relate even more horror stories about the little girls she had seen buried alive, beaten, abandoned, and mistreated by the painful process of foot binding. All of the women missionaries spoke with one voice about how terrible it was simply to hear the shrieking of girls and women as they walked the streets. An almost endless din filled the streets and distressed them to distraction because their efforts seemed so futile.[253] Mrs. Netland, now home in Minnesota, wrote of the heart-rending cries of a little girl who followed them to the boat in Shanghai, praying that she could be saved from slavery. She was glad to report that she had been bought by Christians who would care for her kindly, but the scream of another woman who had been sold into slavery she would not forget until she died.[254]

THEA COMES INTO HER OWN

On February 5, 1897, Olava wrote *Børnevennen* to say that Thea was thriving, including a story about some of their recent travels about the area. Borne by bearers who kept a steady pace with the sedan chairs, they enjoyed the country around Dengcheng but were appalled that these men were considered to be little more than beasts of burden. They found it unpleasant, especially when they passed by a temple with idols, which caused their bearers fear.[255] In the next issue, Olava painted a richly textured picture of the country around Taipingdian where they were teaching.

> The cotton was ripe for harvesting, owing to the recent flood, the cotton pods were more or less destroyed. However, the women with their baskets were at work gathering what yet was spared for them. To see a cotton field just as the pods are blooming is very beautiful. The dark green leaves intermixed with the white boll presents an interesting scene.

She went on to say that the women in the country frequently had better feet since their help was needed on the farm.[256] Then she gave one of the few portraits of Thea we have, describing how she appeared to the Chinese when she entered a room. Though her blonde hair was striking to them and provoked much comment, it was mostly her large feet they could not believe. Always the women would say, "Who would marry my daughter if her feet were not small?"[257] This report on their trip was written in English and was clearly written with children in mind. She gives many interesting details on their food: crispy vegetables stir fried in a wok with rice and soup, and plenty of tea.[258]

That April, Thea wrote to one of her favorite groups in America, the girls' society in Dawson, Minnesota, to thank them for the blanket they had sent and to explain more about her life in China.

She told them of her continued good health and described her frequent house calls and work among the women. "We keep trying to teach women to read," she said. "We read a bit, then knit stockings. Our Sunday and weekly women's meetings are well attended."[259] The next day she wrote to *Budbæreren* that a Bible woman from the London Missionary Society had come to help teach the children in their school, singing and praying with them, and talking to them about their souls. Olava and Thea were now trying to teach the young girls to read and sing. Altogether they had seen seven girls baptized in their work, which was cause for rejoicing.[260]

Dawson Sunday school

At the early spring annual conference of the Hauge Synod missionaries in Fancheng, several decisions were made regarding what we would call job descriptions for each of the missionaries. One of the first decisions, however, was how to take care of the children being brought to the station. Mrs. Rønning made a report to the group, arguing for the creation of a children's home. She had taken in one little girl, Lydia, and three little boys, and could not take in more on her own. The women had talked about the problem, she reported, and the group made several recommendations about what to do for the children, something their readers were anxious they do. They recommended: 1) that Lydia should be Mrs. Rønning's responsibility (they would soon adopt the little girl as their own); 2) that the school boys Tang and Xu should be allowed to continue in the school, and the motherless child that had just been taken in by the mission, even if it was almost too much for Hannah, should be cared for by the mission; and 3) that the women along with the chairman should help decide what should be done for the two little school girls they had in their midst as soon as possible. In addition, each missionary had responsibilities in this context. Landahl was to press on with his language studies and find a way to improve the mission in Taipingdian as soon as possible. Thea was to continue with her weekly meetings with the women and house visits until she moved with her husband to start the new station there. Miss Hodnefield was to continue her work while making preparations to move to Dengcheng and Jizenizhong.[261]

There were more descriptions of Thea's work as the year progressed. In a letter to the women in Madison, Minnesota, Mrs. Himle described going with Thea on a house call where they found an old woman dying. The pigs in the house with her created a terrible mess. The old woman was afraid to die and become an evil spirit. Mrs. Himle wrote that the son's wife told Thea to "preach" the gospel to her. Thea began, but the old woman did not understand nor could she concentrate on what she was saying, instead asking Thea how many sons she had and about what she was wearing.[262] Not long after this, Thea wrote home to the women's organization in Dawson, Minnesota. After thanking the women for their support and mentioning her joy in the gospel, she reported the joy she felt sitting on the floor in the house surrounded by a circle of Chinese women and telling them about Jesus, something for which she was highly regarded. Along with her joy in that, she also reported that she had been very sick during the winter but now was in good health, as was her husband who had been spending much of his time studying the language. While she was writing the letter, Landahl and her brother were in Taipingdian repairing and remodeling a house where they could live.[263] By the time the Landahls were ready to move to Taipingdian, the summer heat was beginning. Halvor, who had worked hard on the station there, was dreading it because his fever had come back, not uncommon for people with malaria before there were drugs to treat it. Despite his fevers, he was planning to build another house in the Liangyang Mountain, where they could go in the summer heat to find relief. He figured the lot cost about $30 and the house with three rooms would cost about $250. For this he urged their supporters to send money so the house could be built as soon as possible, even if it was erhaps an extra burden. For the sake of the mission and the missionaries, they needed to proceed quickly. Although he did not mention the health of the missionaries, it was implicit in his request.[264] Thea was among those whose health suffered the most from the heat, and she needed such a place simply to survive. On July 7, 1897, Himle reported that the Rønnings, Landahls, and Miss Hodnefield had gone to the mountain cabin, even if it was not quite finished, given Rønning's continuing struggle with the fever.[265]

It appears from these later accounts that Thea's ministry was growing and that the Chinese trusted her enough to make use of her skills. The clearest evidence of this is a letter she wrote from Fancheng, an extensive report on her work with women. Saying it was her gift to visit the women in their homes, she used the opportunity to see what kind of a situation there was in the family. Often it filled her heart with compassion, even as it seemed to be an almost hopeless calling, given the need. They would tell her when she spoke to them of heaven and hell that they were already living in hell. She then told a long story about the daughter-in-law of their teacher, Mr. Yang, who came to her meeting with the women in a home. She was unusually beautiful, Thea said, and very intelligent. She asked many questions—not much about the faith, but about Thea, her clothes, and how they were made. Thea explained they were spun and woven on a machine, which amazed the young woman. Her father-in-law had told her that the missionaries were good people and could be trusted and were especially clean and washed. As their relationship grew, Thea began to teach her about the Bible, planning to teach her how to read the Chinese characters common in Scripture. To her surprise, the woman, only nineteen, could read quite well. The young woman returned to her birthplace for a month, but then returned quite ill and weak, enough so that both Thea and Hannah went to visit her in her home regularly.

Then it rained, and they could not leave the station to visit her. Suddenly there was a great uproar outside the station and she went out in her sun hat into the swarms of people around two thieves who were being taken into custody by the police. As she was watching this, a woman came and pleaded with her to come and see two people bound fast to a boat and floating in the water. While she was taking in this situation:

> My eyes fell on a man who was lying on the side of the street with his arms over his face, very abject and troubled.

What do you need, I asked, are you sick? He answered, not so sick but I am so hungry. Where are you from, she asked? From Henan,. Our boat tipped over in the river and I alone survived, poor as you see me. I haven't eaten for several days. A woman, who stood there and leaned on a post nearby, confirmed that his words were true. I asked whether or not she could give him a bowl of rice, and I would very soon bring him more. That she could do. After I had visited several other families, I returned home and made sure the hungry man had gotten something to eat.[266]

Several days later, after dealing with an opium smoker lying near the door, Thea and Hannah went to visit Mrs. Yang, the young woman whom they had found to be so intelligent and curious about

Opium den as pictured in the *Kinamissionæren*

the Christian faith. When they got to the house, two women called to them to go into the house where the woman lay, ill and very weak. She had a room far inside the house which was dark and filthy. The family seemed reluctant to let her go in to the room, but Thea insisted, showing she was not ashamed to go into the situation.

This room was in two parts with a bamboo mat; her husband led us in and pointed at her and said, there she lies, pointing to an opening on the one side of the mat. I went in, but it was so dark that for quite a while I could see nothing of her in the bed, but could hear her familiar voice. Two hands took hold of me on my one arm and with a weak voice she invited me in to sit down on the bed. We spoke together a long time. She thought everything was dark and hopeless.

When I stood up to go, she pleaded with me so movingly to stay another hour. "When I am better, can I come and be with you for several days?" Yes, that would be a joy, if you could come to us. Now I could see better and I could see how the room really looked. There was no window to be found; we needed some light coming through the slits between the ceiling and the walls. It looked more like a cave than a bedroom. The bed was right against the wall that was not much taller than the bed. On the one side, where I stood it was so high that I could stand without touching the filthy straw ceiling. At one end of the bed was a bowl with food for animals. At the other end of the bed there was another hole from which came an unusual smell. I asked her husband what on earth that was, and he said, "Our cow is there during the night," as though everything was as it should be.

I asked him clearly to have the place cleaned up so his wife could be better. He promised me to have it done, but the Chinese have no sense for cleanliness.

I did take comfort in the fact that he did care for her when he came in to look at her. It was with a heavy heart that I went home and wondered what could be done to ease her situation and sent her something I thought would cheer her up. That home is not what the Chinese would call poor, but like the homes of many ordinary Chinese.[267]

Sometime later, Hannah and Thea visited Mrs. Yang again, and she was sitting in the front room, still very weak. They were happy to see that she was much better than she had been before. She began to ask them about salvation and where she would go when she died. "I will go to hell," she said. "But you, who know God, will go to heaven. If I become better, and live, I will accept your teaching, so that I too can go to heaven and be saved." With that Thea asked the women reading this letter in their various gatherings to pray for the young woman and her family, that God's Word would triumph over heathenism.[268]

This is quite a different Thea from the one we saw at the beginning of her travels to America and then to China. No longer was she clinging to the station or her brother. Here she takes stock of the situation, sees what needs to be done, and with dispatch gets it done. She also knows the full power of her letters to raise both interest and support back home—a thing so necessary to the survival of their work. At the end of the letter she greets all the friends of the mission, especially the many Ladies Aids in the synod. "Do not forget our own little China mission; do not forget to pray for our work here, that we will not become exhausted, but stay awake, pray, believe and work."[269] Sometime later, after the Landahls had moved to Taipingdian, Hannah reported that Mrs. Yang had now come back to the station to study with Hannah. Hannah thought that she would soon become a teacher for the girls.[270]

TAIPINGDIAN

Church in Taipingdian

By the end of July, the mission at Taipingdian was going well, but the Landahls and the Himles had gone to the cabin in the mountains to escape the heat. Landahl was happy to report that on their last Sunday, they had had a full house, with interested listeners. "We are resting well, sleeping well, eating and drinking well. We have it good!"[271] At the same time that they were at peace, they were hearing of riots and unrest going on around China, especially in Laohekoo, where the Norwegians had their mission. They were rejoicing also that they were being successful and the Chinese there were getting rid of their idols—a good sign, although one could never predict what would happen in times of unrest. Because of the crowded conditions of the cities, a riot could be fomented in any moment, and the missionaries were well aware of that.

During the heat of the summer in 1897, the missionaries made use of their retreat in Sje-liang frequently. The men would leave their families there and go down to the cities to check on how things were going. Both Halvor and Carl complained of the oppressive heat, but were looking ahead to future baptisms after the heat would break. Of interest is that they are now passing out copies of Luther's *Small Catechism* in Chinese as part of the instructions for baptism. One man to whom he gave the little book had been reading the Gospel of John, especially chapter fourteen. The man, Liu, read the book and came back with several who also wanted to have it. They had read it aloud to each other, and they were struck by it so much so that they wanted to become Christians.[272] Carl and Thea were at Sje-liang for two weeks and found the air to be fresh and healthful. From there they would be leaving to continue building the station in Taipingdian. They took with them the oldest son of the Himles, Edwin, while his parents traveled back to Hankow to visit the graves of their children, consult a doctor concerning Mrs. Himle's health, and meet Miss Fugleskjel, who was arriving soon. The fact that Edwin loved being with the Landahls speaks well for the couple.[273]

The station at Taipingdian seemed to flourish under the care of the newlyweds, and everyone who saw them commented on their good health, somewhat surprising after the recent brush with death and Thea's continuing poor health before her marriage. Especially Carl and Halvor had worked hard building the station where they were to do their work. By Halvor's count, he had been building every year since he came: the station in Hankow, in Fancheng, now in Taipingdian, plus a hospital, several chapels, etc. While he was tired of such work, he did have to say that this work involved him in projects where he had to speak with the Chinese in their language about practical things, even as he could bring them the gospel of Jesus Christ. "When evening comes, I am so tired I don't manage to read very much. If I do read too late, I have a terrible headache the next day."[274]

Because Taipingdian was only thirty miles from Fancheng, the Rønnings visited the new couple in the new station several times. Halvor described a visit they made to their sister and brother-in-law with a charming letter about the trip. Nilius rode a small donkey, Hannah was carried in a sedan chair, and Halvor rode on a horse. The three of them caused much curiosity among the Chinese. Because they had had to get up so early, Nilius fell asleep and had to be taken in the sedan chair while Hannah rode the donkey. Hannah on the little donkey evoked comments and interest until she fell off the animal, much to the amusement of the Chinese. Hannah began riding the horse, and Halvor walked alongside. When they came to a small town and rode through the market, where thousands of people were standing, Nilius became panicky and began screeching. Halvor had to gather up all his courage and tell the crowds, politely, to move back so they could proceed. They responded well, which caused Halvor wonder—three years before he had been stoned by those in the city. As they entered it, they remarked on the greetings they were receiving. They were also thrilled at the reception the missionaries received from the people, especially the Landahls. Although Thea had gone the same way some time before, Hannah with Nilius attracted far more people. Their route was the same as pilgrims on a pilgrimage to the temple of Odansan. The flags the pilgrims carried were pure white with bright red characters, along with the sounds of drums pounding. The pilgrims fell to their knees and bowed their heads three times toward the earth and said some words. They had come from Nanlofoh, which was 200 miles away. Along the road they made offerings of paper. This as usual caused the missionaries some angst because of their deep commitment to converting the Chinese, but they were becoming more and more accustomed to it.

At the end of 1897, Thea and Hannah seemed to be doing well. They wrote a joint letter for the Ladies Aid in Madison, Minnesota, one of the main Hauge Synod congregations, to thank the group for sending them a check for $19.80, which they divided into two parts. After their usual edifying pieces on God's great mercies, they began telling the women in Madison about their work. They had gotten knitting needles from the women in Minnesota and were teaching the Chinese women to knit. While the older women, whose eyes were often bad, found it difficult both to knit and read, the younger ones were excited to learn both skills. These women attended the Sunday services as well as the knitting sessions. While they were teaching the women how to knit and read, Halvor and Landahl were planning to buy a lot where they could build a hospital or at least a clinic. With that they bid adieu to the women in Madison, and said they probably would not be writing during the dog days of summer which were hard upon them at the time.[275]

Landahl had almost finished his remodeling, which had been a most exhausting process. Now it was almost done. They hoped to build a school among other things. Although the Landahls had been very busy remodeling the house and building, as the Rønnings had approached the Landahl's dwelling, they realized it was the first anniversary of their wedding. When they got there, both young couples praised the Lord for all the good they had received through the marriage. After dinner, the Rønnings left quickly on the boat for Fancheng. The trip was only four hours and when they arrived, just about dusk, they were happy to see Olava at the station with Nilius where they joyfully greeted them.

Now that the Landahls had moved, the work in Fancheng for the Rønnings kept them busy in a way they had not been before with Thea and Landahl there. Therefore, they looked forward to the coming of Miss Fugleskjel, whom the Himles had gone to meet in Hankow. For Hannah it would be a pleasure to greet her and have another person to help her with the tasks of their station. Given the short distance between the two stations, Thea was able to come back to their place more frequently than might have been the case if they had been farther apart. She was especially eager keep in contact with Olava whose friendship she cherished and must have missed now that they were apart.

Taipingdian mission station

As the Landahls were settling into their station in Taipingdian, they felt obligated to tell their readers what the new place was like. Toward the end of the year, Landahl wrote a descriptive letter about the city and their station. The town was a lovely small city, a market center, where the people were used to trading and driving hard bargains. It had been a center for theater and a city with a long history which could be traced back almost 500 years. What people gathered around, he said, were the theaters and the temples, mostly Buddhist, but also Confucion, Taoist, and Nanlofo temples, where they worshiped idols. The city had one bank and one banker, two mandarins, and six elders. In addition there were police, soldiers, and many opium smokers. The mission station was on the main street, and everyone who came in to the city from the east gate went by their place. In dry weather the streets were easily passable and in the wet they were almost impossible. It was surrounded by walls. However, during the floods the water would flow over the town, which always wreaked havoc on the population. Farms in the area were extremely fruitful with wheat, corn, barley, and many fields of rice, sweet potatoes, cabbage, and other vegetables. The farmers were probably better off, Landahl supposed, than the city people. Terrible for all the Chinese, however, was opium addiction, he added.[276]

Olava Holdnefeld

Olava, who was still with the Rønnings in Fancheng, had been to visit Thea on her way to the Norwegian mission in Laohekoo. She thought the Landahls had built a nice home and that things were going well. They were teaching Edwin Himle his ABCs so he could surprise his parents when they returned with Miss Fugleskjel from Hankow. While Thea was doing well, the Chinese women in the area, curious as always, nearly overwhelmed her with their visits. To give her some relief, Olava took her with them to Laohekoo where they could enjoy the hospitality of the Norwegians there. During their stay, they received the message that the station was being threatened with destruction by fire because the missionaries had saved a young girl from her mother-in-law's rage. Overcome with despair, the young woman had thrown herself into a fire. She was saved from the fire by her brother-in-law. Mrs. Johnson took the girl and wrapped her in a thick wool blanket and held her. Immediately she went to sleep. Soon the mother-in-law, who figured the girl would come to the missionaries because she had been there frequently, found her and threatened to burn down the station. Although the missionaries—the Johnsons, Thea, and Olava—felt anxious about the threat, they prayed that God would watch over them, retired to bed, and went to sleep immediately. About midnight, Thea was awakened by screeching and footsteps outside the window on the street. It was so disturbing to them they prepared to flee, however when they sent some servants out to see if there was a fire burning in the area they found nothing. For the women, this was a miracle of God's great kindness to them in hearing their prayers.[277] A similar incident happened when the Landahls, just after their Sunday services were finished, found an old woman outside the church, weeping and unable to ask for help because she was so frightened and cold. She had been picked out of the river by two men in a boat, but with her in it, the boat tipped and she escaped. She was wet and cold. They had no time to think what to do. They immediately lit a fire in the schoolhouse so she could warm herself and then found clothes for her, which they had to buy for seventy-five cents. Later she told them she had gone through the town asking for help, but no one would help her except for a banker's son who gave her a little cash to buy food. She had even gone to a temple to find help, but none was given. "They are hard, unmerciful, and unloving," Landahl said, referring to their idols.[278] He then thanked the women's groups for providing them with the means to clothe the naked and feed the hungry. "Your treasures are laid up in heaven," he concluded.

The work in Taipingdian continued and flourished. So many women came to visit Thea that she was completely occupied with them. According to Chinese custom she had to welcome them with hospitality. If she had not, Carl and Thea might have suffered consequences. They were, however, loved by the people in the town who gave them a plaque honoring them for their contributions to the neighborhood. Landahl quoted a Chinese saying that if you bind your daughter's feet hard she will learn to stay at home. In spite of their small feet, he wrote, many women came to greet Thea.[279] Finally the stress of this hospitality made her ill. On Christmas Eve, Thea was very sick. Too much work and too much zeal for the heathen was always a danger to the health of the missionaries, especially Thea. After Christmas that year, Landahl wrote that the Himles were coming to pick up Edwin, who had enjoyed his time with them and they with him.[280]

After the New Year, Thea had recovered and was continuing her Sunday school teaching and women's meetings.[281] The couple continued to host many visitors and also tried to teach the Chinese the Christian faith with some success. They had gone to Fancheng to visit the Rønnings, as well as meet Miss Fugleskjel again—Carl at least had known her in America. The couple was eager to see her get started in her Chinese and learn where she might be placed for her service. On February 22, 1898, the Landahls reported they were both well despite the stress of their work, and that the number of Chinese who came to see and hear what they were teaching and preaching was increasing.

Soon it was time to attend the annual meeting of the Mission Society which was to be held in Fancheng that year.[282] The Landahls left for the meeting with a good report on their work. Everyone at the conference commented on their glowing health, even though Landahl seemed a bit weak. Thea, on the other hand, had never looked or felt better. One suspects that, in the modest language of this period and these people, Thea was probably pregnant, though it was never mentioned. In any event, her work was flourishing. At the meeting every missionary reported on their work. Thea's report stressed once more her deep concern for the women of China. When it happened that a woman came to the station and did not hear the gospel of Jesus Christ, it was like a wound to her heart, she reported. She and Hannah, especially, but also Olava, had taken great care to visit the women who came to their meetings in their own homes, she noted with some pride. Along with her visits to the women in their home, she had also helped Hannah with her classes—especially those in which she was teaching the Chinese women how to read. In addition, of course, she was always studying the language. Together she and her husband Carl were reading through the epistles of Paul in Chinese, along with the books of Job, Revelation, and a textbook on Chinese.

In addition, Thea spoke of the sadness of having to leave Fancheng and her family there, but also the joy of being able to work in a new field which was a great challenge. "The Lord has opened new ways for us."[283] She then described how Landahl would preach on Sunday morning, and in the afternoon many women would return to her meetings where she had a very set agenda: tell about the living Lord, a constant theme of hers, through a Bible story, a parable, or a miracle of Jesus. While it interested them as they were listening to her, she admitted, they would forget as they went back to their own homes. To teach, she realized, she had to study on her own and get to know the truths of the Bible more deeply than she had before. This she could do, however, because of the need. Since the Lord had granted her excellent health during the first year of her marriage, she had made many good friends in Taipingdian. She concluded her report with the prayer that God would grant them in the coming year more love, faith, energy, persistence, and devotion for the souls of the Chinese. "Pray for us, dear sisters and brothers, that the harvest will be great."[284]

That was the third week in March. Two days after the conference, on March 22, she complained of a headache, but it did not seem unusual. Then, just as everyone was retiring, Landahl burst into the Rønnings' room to tell them that Thea was so ill he did not think she would survive the night. The Rønnings and the Himles rushed to her bedside and found her in a dreadful agony of cramps and convulsions. Himle diagnosed it as meningitis. Hannah would write later that she would never forget the night they were called from sleep by Landahl. She had been so well, Hannah remarked, as did Landahl in a later report. She had a terrible first attack of cramps, and then, Landahl wrote, her eyes were clear, and patience and resignation shone in them. Together they thanked God for how wonderful it was to be a child of God and then sang one of her favorite hymns, *"Jeg ved en Ven som til mig smiler"* (I know a friend who smiles at me). "It was beautiful to see my dear Thea standing at heaven's door," Landahl commented. "When we want to complain or ask why me, he could only answer God's ways are not our ways, and then thank God for that our dear Thea is now at home, and it is ours to journey on."[285] In all, she had seven attacks, each of greater intensity. At 6:20 Wednesday morning, March 23, 1898, she died. Her last words were "Will" (her name for Carl) and "heaven." The missionaries knelt beside her bed and praised God that she had come out of the great tribulation and gone home to God. Hannah described the funeral later as a testimony to the Chinese how Christians faced death. After a service in Norwegian in the Fancheng missionary home, they held a service in Chinese for her in the chapel. For her funeral they dressed her in a creamy Chinese silk dress and laid her in a Chinese coffin. The procession to the grave was led by children singing a funeral song. As they put her tenderly to rest in a Chinese grave, the children continued to sing hymns. They buried her, according to the sketchy records, in a little plot beside their clinic in Fancheng.[286]

Mrs. Himle wrote: "She had given her life in the Master's service. The time was not long, but God does not measure in time, but by the faithfulness of the heart. Several hundred people were at the funeral. Missionary Mattson spoke in Chinese. The mission children led the casket singing. After the burial we sang a song in Norwegian and Chinese. It made an impression on the Chinese to see a Christian burial."[287] Landahl said that when he told a young Chinese boy about Thea's death, tears began to roll down his cheeks. For the boy she had been something of a mother, and now that she was gone, he said, he wanted to believe in her God so he could go be with her in heaven.[288]

Fancheng Cemetary

The April 1, 1898, volume of *Kinamissionæren* carried the announcement of Thea's death in its conventional form, too frequently used that year, a picture surrounded by a dark black line and a cross. Later numbers carried tributes to her from the missionaries. They all noted how deeply Thea felt the need of the Chinese women. Mrs. Himle wrote, "I remember having asked her if she was not homesick and longing for America, and she answered, 'Oh, yes, it would certainly be nice to see friends, but when I think of the great opportunities for work and all there is to do, I have no wish whatsoever to go home.'"[289]

Her death was the most difficult loss that Olava Hodnefield had sustained to that time in her life, she wrote later. "To think that Thea would never again feel China's warm sun on her cheeks," she

Announcement of Thea's death

wrote. "Her place is empty. We need workers."[290] The two of them had been friendly companions in their work, and the loss of Thea must have been devastating to Olava, who continued as a missionary for years to come and was among the founders of the Hauge Synod's national women's organization, The Mission Dove Society. When Pastor Brøhaugh, the president of the China Mission of the Hauge Synod, made his annual report to the convention in Red Wing, Minnesota, that June, he remarked that Thea had won entry into the hearts of the women of Taipingdian, and we "rejoiced that a blessed work would unfold in our mission."[291]

Expressions of grief came from all quarters of the Hauge Synod and others who supported the China Mission. It was a topic of conversation through the summer and fall of that year. The girls and women who supported Thea heard of her death in a variety of ways, through the grapevine and through the letters published in the magazines, *Kinamissionæren* and *Budbæreren*. Because of the letters she had sent home, and references to her in the letters from others in China, the readers had come to love and care about her as they had for the others in the mission.

After some time, Olava wrote a letter once more expressing her grief over the loss of Thea. As if to bring her voice back into the conversation, she quoted a letter Thea had written two years earlier, after her illness and her honeymoon in the retreat in the mountains: "We are hoping to come to Fancheng soon, but probably not before November. You should be here, in the woods around us. They are lovely, with high mountains around us. We can hear the brook trilling down the mountain because everything around us is still. How wonderful to know that nature speaks to us of God's good works for us."[292]

One can clearly see in these letters her growth from a young, hesitant woman to one confident in her powers. It was probably to be expected that a young woman could grow into a confident and effective leader with abilities to effect change in her mostly hostile context in China. Although Thea Rønning was by no means the most important woman missionary to China from the Norwegian-Americans, she does stand as an emblem of the life of the women missionaries from that time. Having felt the call to the suffering women in China and supported by women at home who were helping the mission in the regular meetings in America, she nurtured the vital link between mission circles and the mission fields with her warm and descriptive letters of the work she and Olava were doing among the Chinese women. We have some idea where she got the idea to be a missionary, but not exactly. And we can be fairly certain that her call to be a missionary was quite clear, although she does not tell exactly how that happened in any of the sources we have. It is clear that both her Norwegian religious experience and her life in Minnesota offered her plenty of role models so that she could go to China with, what appears to be, confidence. Her private letters and the public letters she wrote for the magazines of the church by themselves give an intimate and rich portrait of her life and work in China.

Her relating of her experiences in China to the women in America elicited warm and concerned responses from the American churches. Their responses show that the bonds of womanhood could transcend national and cultural boundaries because women understood their sisterhood. They sealed that sisterhood with prayers and gifts of worldly goods, understanding that it was the mundane action of sewing quilts or cooking a meal that could have a direct and merciful impact on women far across the seas. As one group of little girls wrote, "We are three girls in Dawson and we are sending $5.00 to China. It ain't much but it is what we have so that the Chinese can hear about Jesus." They may all be gone now, but the sisterhood which Thea helped to nurture lived on in them, and still lives, as we begin to understand and acknowledge what these women did for their Lord and succeeding generations, both here and in China.

AFTERWORD

While the story of Thea, of course, ends with her death, there are others in this account whom the readers may want to read more about.

Carl Landahl continued to work in China. Even as the funeral and mourning were proceeding for Thea, *The China Missionary* records that the Hauge Synod was sending another woman missionary, Alice Holmberg (1879-1961). She left Seattle for Shanghai, following something of the same route Carl traveled on his way to China. It was not long before she arrived in Fancheng, ready to begin her work as a missionary. A Swedish-American who attended Augustana College in Rock Island, she was an educated and gifted woman whom Carl soon married and with whom he had seven children.

Halvor and Hannah continued their work in China, with a long furlough to Norway and America during the time of the Boxer Rebellion in 1900. Hannah died of sprue in 1907 and was buried in the same cemetery in Fancheng where Thea had been buried nine

Hannah Rønning's funeral

years earlier. She had become president of the Mission Dove Society, the Hauge Synod's women's organization, which she chaired until her death.

Halvor left China in 1907 because he had a large family to which he needed to devote his full attention. He went to Canada, around the Edmonton area, where a seminary classmate had bought him land and his brother-in-law, Tom Rorem, had built him a home. His sister in Norway planned to come to help raise the children, but illness prevented her coming. Soon a young woman, Gunhild Hørte, came to take care of the children. Halvor and she fell in love, and he married her. In 1913, he filed a claim for a farm in the Peace River district. His letters to Minnesota drew people to come and build a community there. While farming, he served several congregations in both Saskatchewan and Alberta, but he never returned to China. He continued to serve the church as a pastor and evangelist, preaching the gospel of salvation to any who would hear. In 1940 he was awarded an honorary doctor of divinity degree from St. Olaf College, where he frequently preached and led meetings. He died in 1950 after a long life of service to the Lord he had followed from Norway to China to Canada.

His son, Chester, followed him to the mission field but returned and became the president of the Lutheran college in Edmonton and later the head of the Canadian legation to Maoist China. His major effort was an attempt to negotiate the end to the Vietnam War. He continued in the foreign service, serving as the Canadian ambassador to Iceland and Norway. After the Bamboo Curtain was opened in 1983, he returned with his daughter to China, although he was beginning to suffer the effects of Alzheimer's disease. His daughter wrote a charming account of that trip in which he recognized and was recognized by many of his childhood friends from Fancheng.

The family cherishes its interest in this heritage, as does the Rorem family remember Hannah. The Rorems, another distinguished family from the Hauge Synod, have continued to produce leaders for the church, among them Paul Rorem, editor of the *Lutheran Quarterly*.

Mrs. Gidske Himle died in 1899, not long after Thea. Himle continued his work in China as something of a medical missionary and pastor. In 1902 he wrote a book on the Boxer Rebellion from the point of view of the Norwegian-Americans there.

Marie Fugleskjel died before the turn of the century.

Daniel Nelson and his wife continued their work until he was shot during an altercation in the mid-1920s.

Of these original missionaries it was Olava Hodnefield who survived the longest. Her story is also worth telling, but it is a much longer story, and the sources are harder to track down. As almost the sole survivor of that first generation of women missionaries, she was a testimony not only to her own grit and determination, but to the great sacrifices of all these young Scandinavian-Americans of the Hauge Synod who gave of themselves so that the Chinese people might hear about the Jesus they so loved and wanted to served.

APPENDIX

Ole Syverson Nestegaard's reputation is mixed and confusing at the least. Given his behavior in the Boxer Rebellion when he was housed in the British legation, the historical records are either confused or silent on his ending. Those who knew him, and especially Thorstein Himle in his book on the Boxer Rebellion, *Guds Veie Med et Gjenstridigt Folk: En historisk Beretning,* give Nestegaard credit for raising up the concern for China among the Norwegians and Norwegian-Americans. There was no question that his work on behalf of the Chinese mission was pivotal in the establishment of the China mission from both America and Norway. Trying to follow his peripatetic journeys hither and yon is almost impossible. One can be sure that if there was something happening in the China mission, he was there. The fact that he left the China mission for Mongolia is telling, suggesting he did not thrive when under any kind of supervision or collaboration at all.

While it is clear that he spurred interest in China, his character was always something of an issue. People who had once found him to be a spiritual presence and leader finally began to note that he had not received approval from such luminaries as Hudson Taylor. His emotional reconciliation with Østby in Minnesota during the 1893 meeting of Hauge's Synod, while moving, did not last. To make matters worse, his biographers, understandably, frequently confuse him with his younger brother, Ole Syverson Nestegaard the younger. The biography that I have presented above is, I think, fairly accurate, even if Norlie, who must have heard of the man from those who actually knew him, seems to confuse them as well. While Norlie was usually to be trusted, it is not surprising he got these two brothers confused. This is a caution as one tries to reconstruct their activities. It may be simply that he got the names wrong and his biography of the younger Nestegaard is actually the biography of the elder.

When Hauge's Synod began to cast aspersions on the elder for not being Lutheran, he went to the leaders of Augsburg Seminary who examined him and found him to be Lutheran enough. After that ruling, at a meeting of the China Mission Society, the members decided to send him out as their missionary. He went to China and then to Mongolia, where he and his younger brother established a mission. He was soon fired by the society, and his younger brother resigned in protest. One hears little about him after this until the Boxer Rebellion when he was in Beijing and his station was destroyed by the rebels. Along with many other missionaries, he found refuge in the British legation where his mental condition was so unstable that he was kept under watch. During this time he escaped and went to the Chinese who had respect for people who had lost their minds, thinking them to be in close contact with the spirit world. While he was with the Chinese, he told them much about the situation in the legation, its exact measurements and defensive arrangements and advised them how to shoot more accurately.

Even the Chinese began to weary of him, and he was returned to the Westerners with the help of the young man Chong Li Yamen, who had gone from the legation. Nestegaard would later report to his embassy that during the war he was captured by the Boxers and "held in a wretched prison, with chains on my hands and feet and throat, but because I was a Norwegian and had not been part of those who wanted to wage war on China, Prince Tuan spared my life." Which country he was from made little difference to his captors, some of whom did wish to kill him for treason, but on account of his mental state, they chose to release him back to the Europeans. When those in the legation heard he had betrayed them and had told the Chinese to shoot lower, many wanted to sentence him to death for treason, but Minister Edwin Hind Crogers (1843-1907) spared him. From that time he was put under even stricter watch.

When he heard that Chung Li Yamen was going to return to the Chinese again, he said, "I will go with him." When Brooks asked him what he would do there, he said, "I will find a call." So the morning of June 20, Nestegaard put on his Norwegian cassock and collar, expecting to go with the Chinese man. Despite Brooks' most serious objections, he went. He had scarcely left when he heard that the German minister had been killed with Chung Li Yamen and he decided to return to the legation.

Among the things his Chinese captors found in his effects was an apology to the Russian minister for having exposed himself to the minister's wife. These details occur over and over again in contemporary accounts, so it is difficult to say they did not happen. Most missionaries from the British and American cultures could not say his name, so it is not spelled correctly or even the same in the several accounts there are of the time. Most of them called him "Nasty Guy."

On August 1, 1901 the Swedish-Norwegian consul sent him home from Shanghai. From there he disappeared. Despite that, the historians of Hauge's Synod mission credit him with raising awareness of the need in China. Along with many pioneers, no matter how daft, he had the courage and lack of concern for his own safety to make a huge difference.

ENDNOTES

1. Mungello (2005), 37. Since Italians, Spaniards, Germans, Belgians, and Poles participated in missions too, the total of 920 probably only counts European Jesuits, and does not include Chinese members of the Society of Jesus.
2. Kenneth Scott, *Christian Missions in China*, 83.
3. Hudson Taylor, *China: Its Spiritual Need and Claims*.
4. "H. N. Rønnings Biografi," *Kinamissionæren* 2 (1892), 86.
5. The list of those who returned is a remarkable testimony to the closeness the pioneer pastors felt to their homeland: Ove J. Hjort, August Weenaas, Ulrik Vilhelm Koren, Lauritz Larsen, H. A. Preus, etc.
6. "H. N. Rønnings Biografi," *Kinamissionæren* 2 (1892), 85.
7. Ibid.
8. Ibid.
9. "Thea Rønnings Biografi," *Kinamissionæren* 2 (15 April 1892), 113-114.
10. "Rønnings Biografi," 87.
11. Nils Nilson Rønning, *A Summer in Telemarken and Some Character Sketches* (Minneapolis: The Northland Press, 1903), 103
12. Weenaas, *Livserindringer Fra Norge og Amerika. Biblioteca Norvegiæ Sacræ XII*, (Bergen: A. S. Lunde & Co., Forlag), 180.
13. N. N. Rønning, "Det er ikke greit at være nykommer," *Bara for Moro* (Minneapolis: K. C. Holter Company, 1913), 12.
14. Miss Guinness was the daughter of evangelist Henry Grattan Guinness D. D. (1835 –1910), a good friend of Taylor. She sailed as a single woman to China in 1888 just after the 100 had followed Taylor's call for a 100 missionaries in 1887. Her writings about missionaries and their work in China, especially, challenged thousands of young people to answer the call to be missionaries. The Elliotts went to Ecuador after reading her books.
15. "Thea Rønnings Biografi," *Kinamissionæren* 2 (15 April, 1892), 113-114.
16. Ibid., 114.
17. N. N. Rønning, "Det er ikke greit at være nykommer," *Bara for Moro* (Minneapolis: K. C. Holter Company, 1913), 6.
18. There are no pictures surviving from this period.
19. Letter from Thea Rønning to her family (7 June 1887).
20. Letter from Thea Rønning to her family describing their journey across the Atlantic. Nd.
21. Letter from Thea Rønning to her family, (17 July 1887).
22. Ibid.
23. Letter from Thea to her family, (7 August 1887).
24. Letter from Thea to her family, (16 November 1887).
25. Ibid.

26 Ibid.
27 Letter from Thea to her family, (26 February 1888).
28 Ibid.
29 Ibid.
30 Thea's letter home, fall, 1888?
31 Thea's letter home, May? 1888.
32 *St. Paul Daily Globe*, (5 September 1888), 3.
33 *Omaha Daily Bee*, (7 September 1888), 2.
34 Thea's letter home, (12 December 1888).
35 Gustava Kielland, *Erindringer fra mit liv*. Forord af professor dr. Ludvig Daae, (Steen: Kristiania, 1902), 8.
36 *Solør Congregation History*, ALC Archives, Luther Seminary.
37 This was fairly common for pastors to do. It was a running argument in my parsonage home when my father would excoriate the ladies aids for thinking only of dinners and food events to raise money for missions; he thought they should just give the money, which, my mother would retort, they did not have because women did not earn money outside the home.
38 History of the Tabitha and Lydia Ladies Aid, Cottonwood, Iowa, ALC Archives, Luther Seminary.
39 Stanley Smith, Dixon Hoste, William Cassels, Montague Beauchamp, Cecil Polhill-Turner, Arthur Polhill-Turner and Charles T. Studd.
40 Arne Boyum, "President's Report to Hauge's Synod," *Budbæreren* 15 (15 August 1883), 114.
41 *Budbæreren* 17 (23 September, 1885), 367.
42 Bagnall, *China's Millions,* 13 (January 1888), 12.
43 *China's Millions*, 13 (June 1888), 66-69.
44 Although I have tried to find this volume, it does not appear to have survived the years.
45 Hatlestad, *Luthersk Kirketidende* 3 (February 1886), 28.
46 Herman Preus, *Evangelisk Lutherske Kirketidende* 13 (26 February 1886), 135.
47 *Budbæreren*, 19 (5 November 1887), 714
48 *Lutheraneren*, 22 (3 March 1888), 67
49 *Missionary Review of the World*, 1 (May 1888), 345-350.
50 *Lutheraneren,* 22 (29 September 1888), 308.
51 *Missionary Review of the World* 2 (February 1889),113.
52 *Missionary Review of the World* 2 (February 1889), 114.
53 Ibid.
54 Ibid.
55 Lucy Rider Meyer, *Missionary Review of the World* 1 (December 1888), 940.
56 *Kina under Korset: En Beretning om Næstegaard=Brødrenes Mission bland Kineser, Mongoler og Tibetaner*. (Minneapolis: Den Forenede Kirkes Trykkeri, 1895).
57 Several sources refer to Ahlberg as being at the mission school, but he does not appear in the histories of the current school.
58 Ibid. 43.
59 *Budbæreren,* 21 (5 October 1889), 638.

60 *Kina under Korset*, (Den Forenede Kirkes Trykkeri: Minneapolis 1895), 54
61 *Lutheraneren* 24 (12 July 1890), 228.
62 Miss Guinness, "Et Nødskrig fra Kina: et brev fra Frøken Guinness i Shektien til Regions Beyond," 24 *Lutheraneren* 24 (22 February 1890), 67.
63 This was not an uncommon age for boys to leave Norway, but I am not quite sure whether to believe the reports about this.
64 Ibid., 24 (2 August 1890), 493.
65 *ELK*, (2 August 1890),493.
66 Thea to family, 28 August 1890.
67 Østby, *Kinamissionæren* 1 (1 January 1891), 8.
68 *Budbæreren* 23 (*14 March 1891*), 173-174.
69 *Kinamissionæren* 1 (1 April 1891), 55-56.
70 *Budbæreren* 23 (27 June, 1891), 404.
71 O. S. Nestegaard the elder, *Budbæreren* 23 (11 August 1891), 492.
72 *Budbæreren* 23 (29 June, 1891), 403.
73 "En forandring," *Kinamissionæren* 1 (15 August 1891), 177.
74 *Budbæreren*, 23 (22 August 1891), 543.
75 *Solør Congregational History*, 6, ALC Archives, Luther Seminary.
76 Miss Hannah Rorems Biografi, *Kinamissionæren* 1 (15 December 1891), 304-305
77 Thea Rønnings Biografi, *Kinamissionæren* 2 (15 April 1892), 114.
78 Hannah Rorems Biografi, 304
79 *Kinamissionæren* 1 (1 November 1891), 262-263.
80 *Kinamissionæren* 1 (1891), 258.
81 Thea to her sister Mari, (13 October 1891).
82 Ibid.
83 Ibid.
84 *Dagbog af Thea Rønning, Reisen fra America til Kina*, Faribault (28 October, 1891), 1.
85 Ibid.
86 "Halvor Rønnings Dagbog," *Kinamissionæren* 1 (1891), 164.
87 *Dagbog af Thea Rønning, Reisen fra America til Kina*, Faribault (28-29 October 1891).
88 *Kinamissionæren* 1 (1891), 163.
89 Thea's *Dagbog*, Thursday, (29 October 1891).
90 Thea's *Dagbog*, Friday, (30 October l891).
91 Thea's *Dagbog*, (1 November 1891).
92 *Kinamissionæren* 2 (1 July 892), 194.
93 Thea's *Dagbog*, (2 November 1891).
94 Thea's *Dagbog*, (3 November 1891).
95 *Kinamissionæren* 2 (15 July 1892), 209.
96 Thea's *Dagbog*, (6 November 1891).
97 *Kinamissionæren* 2 (15 July 1892), 211.
98 *Halvor Rønnings Dagbog, Kinamissionæren* 2 (1 August 1892), 230.
99 *Halvors Rønnings Dagbog, Kinamissionæren* 2 (15 August 1892), 245.

100. Ibid.
101. Halvor Rønnings, *Dagbog, Kinamissionæren* 2 (1 September 1892), 259
102. Ibid.
103. The Norwegian China Mission had sent nine missionaries, six men and three women: Brantzeg, Knut Sorensen Stokke, Ole Mikkelsen Sama, Ludvig Johnson, Hendrik Seyffarth, Johan Alberth Olsen Skordal, Berthine Aarestad, Britha Nilsdatter Vestervig, Berthine Eriksen.
104. Ibid. *Kinamissionæren* 2 (1892), 285.
105. Thea Rønning, Wuchang, Kina, *Kinamissionæren* 1 (14 December 1891), 70-72.
106. Ibid.
107. Ibid.
108. H. N. Rønning with N. N. Rønning *The Gospel at Work*, (Minneapolis: Rønning, 1943), 38-39.
109. Thea Rønning, letter to *Kinamissionæren*, from Wuchang, 1 (14 December, 1891). *Kinamissionæren* 1 (1 March 1892), 70.
110. Péter Vaya, *Empires and Emperors of Russia, China, Korea, and Japan: Notes and Recollections by Monsignor Count Vay de Vaya and Luskod* 1906), 126.
111. Halvor Rønning to Østen Hanson, 5 January 1892, *Budbæreren* 24 (26 March 1892), 196-198.
112. All this page is from her letter of this day. Fra Thea Rønning, Wuchang, Kina, den 26de December 1891, *Kinamissionæren 2 (15 March 1892), 92-94*
113. Ibid. Redaktor, 94.
114. *Kinamissionæren* 2 (1 October 1892), 300.
115. Ibid.
116. Hannah Rønning to Østby, Wuchang, 23 January 1892, *Kinamissionæren* 2 (1 May 1892), 141
117. *Kinamissionæren* 2 (1 January 1892), 8, 25.
118. *Missionary Review of the World*, 2 (February 1889), 113.
119. *Kinamissionæren* 2 (15 February, 1892), 62.
120. *Daily Yellowstone Journal*, (9 August 1888), 2.
121. *Kinamissionæren* , 2 (15 March 1892), 85, 89.
122. Halvor Rønning, *Kinamissionæren* 2 (1 April 1892), 103.
123. *Missionary Review of the World*, 5 (March 1892), 338.
124. Hannah Rønning, May 9, 1892, *Kinamissionæren,* Wuchang, 2 (15 July) 220
125. Johannes Brantzeg, April 1892, *Kinamissionæren 2 (1 July 1892),* 198.
126. *Kinamissionæren* , Gertine (sic) Aarestad, April 25, 1892 *Kinamissionæren,* 201.
127. Halvor Rønning, *Kinamissionæren,* 2 (15 November 1892), 347-348.
128. *Kinamissionæren* (15 January 1893) 27 from Adele M. Fielde, *Pagoda shadows: studies from life in China.*Third edition. Introduction by Joseph Cook. (W. G. Corthell: Boston, 1885).
129. Fielde, "The Extent of a Great Crime," *Pagoda Shadows: studies from life in China*, 38.
130. Thea to Pigeforening, 1 February, 1893, *Kinamissionæren* 3(1 February 1893), 40.
131. Thea to *Budbæreren*, 2 January 1893, *Budbæreren* 3 (March 4, 1893), 134-135.
132. Ibid.

133 Fra Olava Hodnefield, January 26, 1893, Hankow, *Kinamissionæren* 3 (1 April 1893), 106.
134 Fra Oline Hermanson, Hankow, January26, 1893 *Kinamissionæren* 3 (1 April 1893), 107.
135 Fra Oline Hermanson, Hankow, January 26, 1893, *Kinamissionæren* 3 (1 April 1893), 106.
136 Fra Rønning, Hankow, February 8, 1893. *Kinamissionæren* 3 (15 April 1893), 124.
137 Fra Oline Hermanson, 23 April 1893 *Kinamissionæren,* (1 July 1893), 205.
138 Fra Thea Rønning to *Budbæreren* September 2, 1893 (10 July 1893), 548-549.
139 Fra Halvor Rønning 1 August, 1893, Fangcheng *Kinamissionæren, (*1November 1893), 327.
140 Fra Thea Rønning, 28 August 1893 to her parents.
141 Ibid.
142 Oline Hermanson, *Kinamissionæren* 3 (15 August, 1893), 248.
143 Beaver, 113.
144 Fra Halvor Rønning, September 4, 1893, Hankow, *Kinamissionæren* 3 (1893), 329.
145 Ibid.
146 *Mission Review*, 6 (August 1893), 609.
147 *Kinamissionæren* 3 (1 June 1893), 167.
148 Fra Thea Rønning, 3 November, 1893, Hankow, *Kinamissionæren* 4 (15 January 1894), 24.
149 Fra Oline Hermanson, 4 November, 1893, Hankow, *Kinamissionæren* 4 *(*January 15, 1894), 25.
150 Fra Olava Hodnefield, 7 November 1893 Hankow, *Kinamissionæren* 4 (January 15, 1894), 27.
151 *Missionary Review*, 4 (November 1893), 873.
152 *Kinamissionæren* 4 (1 March 1894), 75.
153 Fra Hannah Rønning October 31, 1894, *Kinamissionæren* 5 (12 January 1895), 26-27.
154 Ibid., 3 (15 February 1895), 62.
155 Fra Netland, 10 January, 1894, *Kinamissionæren* 4 (1 April 1894), 99.
156 Fra Mrs. Rønning, February 26, 1894, Hankow, *Kinamissionæren* 4 (1 May1894), 137.
157 *Budbæreren* (5 May 1894), 280.
158 Fra Netland, 29 January 1894, *Kinamissionæren* 4 (1 April 1894), 99.
159 Fra Oline Hermanson, Hankow, January 12, 1894, *Kinamissionæren* 4 (1 April 1894), 90-91
160 Halvor Rønning, Kinamissionen, *Kinamissionæren* 4 (1 June 1894), 162-163.
161 Thea Rønning, Private letter 4 March 1894.
162 Halvor Rønning, *Kinamissionæren* 4 (1 June 1894), 162-163.
163 Referat af Konferentsen i Hankow, 1 July 1894, *Kinamissionæren* 4 (1 July, 1894), 204-207.
164 Thea Rønning, "Til Hauges Menigheds Kvindeforening, Faribault, Minn." *Kinamissionæren* 4 (1 June 1894), 169.
165 Fra Rønning, 28 April 1894, Hankow, *Kinamissionæren* 4 (1 July, 1894), 202.

166 Referat af Konferentsen i Hankow, March 26-28 1894, April 16-19th, 1894, April 28, 1894, *Kinamissionæren*, 204-207.
167 Fra D. Nelson, Hankow, May 14, 1894, *Kinamissionæren* 4 (15 July, 1894), 218.
168 The movie *The Inn of The Sixth Happiness* shows just such a scene when Ingrid Bergman stops to help a boy in the street and the Chinese think she is hurting him and she has to flee from them. In fact, many of the scenes in that movie, although portraying the Sino-Japanese war in the 1930s, are much as the Rønnings report in their letters forty years before.
169 Fra Rønning, Fancheng, June 6, 1894, *Kinamissionæren* 4 (15 August 1894), 247.
170 Thea to her parents and siblings from Fancheng, June 2, 1894. Private letter.
171 "Rønnings Udtrædelseserklæring, Thea Rønnings Udtrædelseserklæring April 9, 1895," *Kinamissionæren* 4 (15 August, 1894), 254-255.
172 "Kinamissionen," *Kinamissionæren* 4 (15 July, 1894), 224.
173 A. O. Oppegaard, Generalmøde, 31 July 1894, *Kinamissionæren* 4 (15 August 1894), 248.
174 Af Brev fra Netland, Fancheng, 10 July 1894, *Kinamissionæren* 4 (1 September 1894), 287.
175 Fra Netland, Fancheng, (8 August 1894), *Kinamissionæren* 4 (15 October 1894), 307-309.
176 Ibid.
177 *Kinamissionæren* 4 (15 November 1894), 344-351.
178 *Budbæreren* 26 (8 December 1894), 774.
179 *Budbæreren* 27 (2 February 1895), 85.
180 *Kinamissionæren* 4 (1 July 1894), 205.
181 Letter from Thea to her family, 1894.
182 *Kinamissionæren* 4 (1 November 1894), 321.
183 Fra Netland, 15 November 1894, Fancheng *Kinamissionæren* 5 (15 January 1895), 21.
184 *Kinamissionæren* 5 (1 January 1895), 6.
185 Fra Olava Hodnefield, Fancheng, 11 October 1894, *Kinamissionæren* 5 (1 January 1895), 5.
186 Fra Oline Netland, October 1894, *Kinamissionæren* 5 (1 January 1895), 4.
187 Fra Thea Rønning, 23 February 1895 *Budbæreren*, 27 (23 February 1895), 118.
188 Fra Hannah Rønning, Fancheng, (31 October 1894), *Budbæreren* 25 (12 January 1895), 28-29.
189 Fra S. T., *Kinamissionæren* 5 (1 March 1895), 60.
190 Frk. Ragnhild Botner, *Kinamissionæren* 5 (15 June 1895), 185. Miss Botner, a Norwegian citizen who studied medicine in Norway, New York, and London, would marry Johan Andreas Olsen Gotteberg in 1899. Her career with her husband in the Hupeh province in China and the Norwegian Mission Society's hospital was long and distinguished, but she disappears from the Hauge Synod's purview after these comments.
191 *Hedningmssionen, Kinamissionæren* 5 (1 July 1895), 205.
192 Gertine Johnsen in *Kineseren*, reprinted in *Budbæreren* 27 (23 February 1895), 116-117.
193 Fra Netland, Kjen geo St., Fancheng, 24 January 1895, *Kinamissionæren* 5 (15 April 1895),117-118.

194 Fra Mrs. Netland, Fan-ch'eng, (4 May 1895), *Kinamissionæren* 5 (15 July, 1895), 215.
195 Fra Thea Rønning, May 4, *Budbæreren* 27 (4 May 1895).
196 Rønning skriver, fra *Budbæreren*, note *Kinamissionæren* 5 (15 July 1895), 222.
197 *Kina under Korset: En Beretning om Næstegaard=Brødrenes Mission bland Kineser, Mongoler og Tibetaner.* (Minneapolis: Den Forenede Kirkes Trykkeri, 1895).
198 Thea Rønning, *Budbæreren* 27 (23 March 1895), 184.
199 *Budbæreren* 27 (23 March 1895), 184.
200 Paul Ofstedal, former head of the China Venture Services, whose daughter married a Chinese man whom she met while working in Beijing, says that his daughter's mother-in-law has a pronounced limp from the practice, even in 2012.
201 Ibid. 27 (13 April 1895), 234.
202 *Budbæreren*, 27 (23 March 1895), 184-186.
203 Ibid.
204 *Budbæreren* 27 (25 May 1895), 326.
205 Thea to *Børnevennen*, Fancheng, 16 April 1895, *Børnevennen*, 18 (23 June 1895), 98.
206 Nestegaard's story is very complicated and worth noting. See appendix 1.
207 "O. S. Næstegaards Beskyldninger," Budbæreren 27 (7 September 1895), 569.
208 Fra Rønning 10 May 1895, Fancheng, *Kinamissionæren* 5 (October 1895), 292.
209 Letter from Thea to her parents, (19 May 1895).
210 Fra Olava Hodnefield, Hankow, (1 July 1895), *Kinamssionæren* 5 (1 September 1895), 272.
211 Letter from Thea to her parents, 19 May 1895?
212 Fra Netland in the president's Report, *Kinamissionæren* 5 (15 November 1895), 343.
213 Fra Sophie Clausen, *Kinamissionæren* 5 (15 December 1895), 379.
214 Letter from Thea to her parents, 19, 27 August 1895.
215 Letter from Olava Hodnefield, (10 January 1896), *Børnevennen* (12 April 1896), 59-60.
216 Letter from Thea to her parents, (28 October 1895).
217 Ibid.
218 Fra Halvor Rønning to *Budbæreren*, 12 October 1895, in *Budbæreren* 27 (7 December 1895), 787.
219 *Børnevennen* (12 January 1896), 6.
220 *Budbæreren* 28 (1 February? 1896), 37.
221 *Ibid*, 72.
222 *Ibid*.
223 *Ibid*, 73.
224 *Budbæreren* 28 (25 April 1896), 266.
225 *Lutheraneren*, (6 February 1896), 81.
226 *Lutheraneren* (2 December 1895), 228.
227 *Budbæreren* 28 (4 April 1896), 219.
228 *Budbæreren* 28 (14 March 1896), 169.
229 *Budbæreren 28 (*3 May 1896), 245.

230 *Børnevennen* 28 (8 November 1896), 180.
231 *Budbæreren* 28 (6 June 1896), 361.
232 *Budbæreren* 28 (13 June 1896), 377.
233 *Budbæreren* 28 (13 June 1896), 378.
234 *Kinamissionæren* 6 (15 January 1896), 22.
235 *Budbæreren* 28 (4 May 1896), 442,
236 Fra Mrs. Himle, 23 July 1896, *Budbæreren* 28 (19 September 1896), 6.
237 Vaccinations against small pox last a long time, but their power does fade so it is possible to contract it years after being vaccinated. Vaccination against the disease was common practice in the Norwegian churches after the Enlightenment when Lady Montagu brought back from her travels in the East the practices which she had observed there. There are two varieties of the disease and it could be that she contracted the minor version of it, or simply chicken pox. She survived it and there is little talk of her being terribly scarred by the disease either.
238 Private letter from Thea to family, n. d. 1896.
239 Fra Rønning, 15 August 1896, *Budbæreren* 28 (17 October 1896), 665.
240 *Budbæreren* 29 (2 January 1897), 13.
241 Ibid.
242 Fra editor, "Fra Broder Landahl," 28 (5 December 1896), 778.
243 Fra Mrs. Landahl, Kin Kiang, 23 October 1896, *Budbæreren* 28 (19 December 1896), 812.
244 Ibid. 91.
245 Fra Landahl, *Budbæreren* 29 (1 May 1897), 284.
246 Fra Landahl *Budbæreren* 29 (22 May 1897), 330.
247 Ibid.
248 Ibid., 204.
249 Fra Landahl, nd, 29 (3 April 1897), 217.
250 Fra Himle *Budbæreren* 29 (20 March 1897), 181.
251 *Budbæreren* 29 (9 January 1897), 28
252 *Kinamissionæren* 7 (15 January 1897), 30.
253 Fra Himle, *Budbæreren* 29 (13 February 1897), 107.
254 Fra Mrs. Netland, *Budbæreren* 29 (15 February 1897), 84.
255 Fra Olava, 5 February1897, *Børnevennen* 20 (16 May 1897), 78.
256 Fra Olava, (23 May 1897), 81.
257 *Børnevennen* (16 May 1897), 78.
258 *Børnevennen* (13 June 1897), 93.
259 Fra Olava Hodnefield, 16 March 1897, *Budbæreren* 29 (9 May 1897), 299.
260 Ibid.
261 Indberetning fra Mrs. Rønning, Missionæreners Konferents i Fancheng, *Budbæreren* 29 (26 June 1897), 411-412.
262 Olava Hodnefield *Budbæreren* 29 (19 June 1897), 393.
263 Fra Mrs. Landahl til Kvindeforeningen i Dawson, Minn, Fancheng 13 April 1897, *Budbæreren*. 29 (17 July 1897), 460.
264 Af Breve fra Kina fra Rønning, Fancheng June 1897, *Budbæreren* 29 (21 August 1897), 539.

265 Fra Th. Himle, 7 July 1897, *Budbæreren* 29 (28 August 1897), 555.
266 Fra Thea Landahl, 3 June 1897, *Budbæreren* 29 (4 September 1897), 572.
267 Ibid.
268 Fra Mrs. Landahl, *Budbæreren* 29 (11 September 1897), 586.
269 Ibid.
270 Fra Mrs. Rønning, 22 November 1897, *Budbæreren* 30 (15 January1898), 42.
271 Fra Rønning, Fancheng 30 July 1897, *Budbæreren* 29 (18 September 1897), 603.
272 *Budbæreren* 29 (16 October 1897), 666.
273 Fra Himles Privatbrev Han River 22 September 1897, *Budbæreren* 29 (6 November 1897), 714.
274 Fra Rønning, 21 October 1897, *Budbæreren* 29 (27 November 1897), 763.
275 Fra Thea and Hannah to Madison Minnesota Ladies Aide, *Budbæreren* (9 October 1897), 952.
276 Fra C. W. Landahl, *Budbæreren* 30 (8 January 1898), 24.
277 Fra Olava Hodnefield *Budbæreren* 30 (29 January 1898), 73.
278 Fra Landahl, *Budbæreren* 30 (29 January 1898), 74.
279 Fra Landahl, *Budbæreren* 30 (5 February 1898), 87.
280 Fra Landahl *Budbæreren* 30 (12 March 1898), 170.
281 Fra Landahl, *Budbæreren* 30 (27 March 1898), 202.
282 Fra Landahl, *Budbæreren* 30 (23 April 1898), 264.
283 Thea's report to the conference, *Budbæreren* 30 (1 June 1898), 423.
284 Ibid.
285 Landahl, *Budbæreren* 30 (20 August 1898), 535-537.
286 Fra Himle, 27 March, 1898, *Kinamissionæren* 8 (1 June 1898), 178-180.
287 Ibid. She was buried on March 26, 1898.
288 Fra Landahl, *Budbæreren* 30 (20 August 1898), 535-537.
289 Alma Himle, (23 March 1898), "In Glory," *Evangeliets seier; festskrift for Hauge synode Kinamissions 25 aars jubilaeum 1891-1916, redigeret af pastor Th. Himle med bistand af pastor H. N. Rønning og pastor A. O. Oppegaard. Udgivet ifølge Synodens beslutning,*130.
290 Fra Olava Hodnefield, Fancheng 31 March 1898, *Budbæreren* 30 (11 June 1898), 378-379.
291 Brøhaugh's report, *Hauges aarsmøde*, Jun 1-8, (1898).
292 Fra Olav Hodnefield to *Budbæreren* 30 (17 September 1898), 601.

PHOTO CREDITS

Page	Credit
6	Gracia at farm—photographer, Oyvind Gullikson
11	Thea Rønning—Luther Seminary Archives (LSA)
13	Hudson Taylor—LSA
17	Matteo Ricci—internet, creative commons
19	CIM Headquarters— creative commons
20	Fredrik Franson—book
21	Reginald Radcliffe—book
23	August Weenaas—Erindringer
24	Geraldine Guinness—creative commons
26	Old church in Bø—author
27	Sofie Reuter Smith—*Pionerer I Skjørter*
28	Geiser ship—creative commons
30	Nils Rønning—LSA
31	Østen Hanson—LSA
34	Thorstein Himle—LSA
35	Dwight L. Moody—creative commons
37	Gustava Kielland—*Erindringer fra mitt liv*, internet
38	Diderikke Ottesen Brandt—LSA
39	Ladies Aid meeting –LSA
42	Stanley Smith—creative commons
43	Hsiu-chi Cheng, Sofie Reuter, and Anna Jakobsen—*Pionerer I Skjørter*
44	Herman A. Preus—LSA
45	Lars Dahle—LSA
49	Ole Syversen Nestegaard the elder—*Kina under Korset*, LSA
51	One hundred missionaries—creative commons
52	Daniel and Anna Nelson—LSA
53	Nestegaard the younger—LSA
54	Ole A. Østby—LSA
56	Rønning and Nestegaard with a family—LSA
57	Sigvald Netland— LSA
59	Thea and Halvor—LSA
60	St. Paul congregation—LSA
61	Solør church—LSA
62	Hannah Rorem—LSA
64	Arendal church—
65	Thea Rønning—LSA Nils & Kjersti Buskerønning— Home of the Rønnings— Church in Bø—
67	"Chinese Bismark"—KM *(Kinamissionæren)*
69	Swedish missionaries—book
70	Hannah Rorem—LSA
78	Shanghai harbor—creative commons
81	Norwegian missionaries in China, 1891—LSA
82	Hankow street—LSA
84	Map of Hauge Synod mission field in China—LSA
85	Hankow—creative commons
86	Halvor and Hannah Rønning—LSA
90	Halvor's letter—LSA
100	Erik Folke—book
101	Griffith John—LSA
103	Missionary house in Hankow—LSA
105	Women spinning yarn—KM/LSA
107	Olava and Oline—LSA
110	Chinese orphange girls—LSA
115	Mr. and Mrs. Nyholm—LSA
118	Women missionaries—LSA
119	Empress Dowager—creative commons
120	Olava Hodnefield—LSA
121	Sun Yatsen and Song Quinling—LSA/KM
122	Norah Nelson—LSA
127	Market in Hankow— Working land near the mission station— Market in Hankow— Missionaries with Hudson Taylor— The door to a Chinese home— Chinese teach with wife and children—
129	Rønning Family in Chinese dress—LSA
131	Cover of *Kinamissionæren*—LSA
137	Marietta Fugleskjel—SA
140	Oline Hermanson Netland—SA
143	Sister Caroline Johnson—LSA
145	Ragnhild Botner—LSA
147	Bound foot—LSA/KM
149	Christian Brøhaugh—LSA
154	Carl Landahl—LSA
156	Gidske Himle—LSA
157	Red Wing Seminary—LSA
160	Hudson Taylor—creative commons
162	Taipingdian congregation—LSA
163	Hannah Rorem Rønning—LSA
168	Lars Kristenson family—LSA
170	Chinese river boat—LSA
174	Johan Skordal—LSA
176	Dawson Sunday school—LSA
179	Opium den—KM/LSA
182	Church in Taipingdian—LSA
185	Taipingdian mission station—LSA
186	Olava Hodnefield—LSA
190	Fancheng Cemetery—LSA
191	Announcement of Thea Landahl's death—LSA
193	Hannah Rønning's funeral—LSA

INDEX

A

Aarestad, Berthine 79, 81, 93, 97, 98, 202n103
Aarflot, Berte Canutte 46
Africa 20, 21, 24
Ahlberg, P. A. 50, 200n57
Albert Lea 158
American Baptist Union 46
American Bible Society 43
Anti-Foreign Riots 66, 109
Anti-Missourian Brotherhood 22, 112, 160
Arendahl congregation 58
Arendal, Norway 20, 21
Argent, William 80
Aspelund, Minnesota 29, 30, 55, 56
Aubol, Carl Otto 160
Augsburg Seminary 22, 23, 112, 151, 197

B

Bagnall, Benjamin 43
Baxter's Mission School 50, 53
Beijing 17, 119, 125, 139, 158, 197, 205n200
Berthemy Convention 158
Bible Missionary Training School 115
Biørn, Ludvig Marinus 22
Bø i Telemark 6, 8, 11
Bø i Vesteraalen 23
Borchgrevink, Christian Doederlein 42
Børnevennen 150, 153, 155, 163, 175
Botner, Ragnild 144, 145, 204n190
Bound feet 16, 17, 24, 58, 95, 104, 106, 108, 147, 148, 187
Boxer Rebellion 78, 85, 111, 153, 163, 193, 194, 196, 197
Boyum, Arne Ellardson 42, 135, 200n40
Bragernæs Church 49
Brandt, Diderikke Ottesen 38
Brandt, Nils Olsen 38
Brandtzeg, Johannes Berg 78, 80-82, 95, 97, 99
British Church Mission Society 75
British Free Methodist Church 74
Brøhaugh, Christoffer Olson 61, 63, 135, 144, 149, 191, 207n291
Brynjulfsen, John A. 112

Budbæreren 42, 51, 55, 57, 60, 92, 134, 137, 144, 146, 149, 155, 167, 172, 173, 176, 191
Buddha 117
Burma 41
Buskerønning, Kjersti 65
Buskerønning, Nils 65
Buxton, Barclay Fowell 75

C

Cambridge Seven Stars 42
Canton, South Dakota 41
Carey, William 41
Catholic 17, 18, 76, 79, 173
Cent Society 160
Chatauqua at Mahtomedi, Minnesota 52
Chicago, Illinois 29, 115
Children's Friend 150, 155
China's Millions 24, 43, 52, 64, 200n42-43
China Inland Mission (CIM) 18, 19, 21, 43, 50, 53, 78, 79, 89, 96, 100, 146, 150, 159
China Mission Society 55, 57, 59, 60, 62, 63, 83, 101, 109, 112, 122, 128, 134, 138, 144, 146, 150, 152, 155, 159, 160, 172, 188, 197, 204n190
Chinese civilization 58, 174
Chinese Evangelical Society 18
Cholera 94, 100, 101, 166, 167
Christiania, Norway (now Oslo) 28
Christiansfeld, Denmark 38
Christmas 33, 50, 85-87, 107, 119, 120, 123, 155, 157-159, 161, 187
Clausen, Sophie 153, 174, 205n213
Clermont, Iowa 61
Columbian Exposition 115
Concordia Seminary 38
Conference 21, 42, 45, 46, 51, 112
Confucian 13-15, 17, 174
Consecration and Blessing 43
Copenhagen, Denmark 28, 60
Crøger, Johannes Christian Thorvald 19, 22, 26
Crookston, Minnesota 53, 54

Index | 209

D

Dahle, Lars 45, 47, 56, 59, 96
Dawson, Minnesota 62, 117, 175-177, 192, 206n263
Deaconess 48, 108
Den-ch'eng 175, 177
Denby, Charles 123, 158, 171
Den Forenede Norsk Lutherske Kirke i Amerika 55
Den norsk-evangelisk Lutherske Kinamissionsforening 55
Dexter, Iowa 63
Dexter, Minnesota 158
Dodge County, Minnesota 24
Dowager Empress Cixi 16, 110, 118, 119, 139
Drammen, Norway 19, 49
Dyer, Maria 18

E

Easter 99, 109
Eistensen, Ingvald 108
Elgin, Lord 15
Erick Folke's Mission 100
Estherville, Iowa 51
Eunuchs 15, 16
Evangelisk Luthersk Tidende 44
Extra-territorial rights 14, 111

F

Fancheng 89, 95, 97, 99, 100, 102, 109, 111-114, 116, 119, 121, 123-126, 128-134, 136, 139, 144, 145, 151, 152, 154-159, 161, 162, 164, 166-169, 172, 176, 178, 183, 185, 186, 188-191, 193, 194
Faribault, Minnesota 24, 28, 29, 32-34, 61, 67-69, 72, 130, 136, 144, 157, 159, 201, 203
Feng shui 136
Fielde, Adelle 104, 105, 108
Folke, Erick 99, 100
Forbidden City 15
Foreign Devils 82, 87, 106, 111, 133, 151
Formosa 151
Franciscans 17
Franson, Fredrik 19-21, 69, 73
Friends of Augsburg 112
Fugleskel, Marietta 104, 118, 137, 139, 183, 185, 186, 188, 195

G

Gaardsmoe, Hans Arneson 151
Ganjing 50
Geary Act 109, 116
Geiser ship 28

Girl babies 25, 58, 105, 153
Gjerstad, Gustav Christianson 61
Great Britain 15
Great Within 15
Green, Customs official 80
Grønsberg, Ole 71
Guangko 173
Gucheng 152
Guinness Taylor, Mary Geraldine 24, 52, 53, 199n14
Gunnersen, Sven Rudolf 22, 23
Gunning, J. A. 135

H

Hallingdal 49
Hamilton County, Iowa 62, 107
Hankow 58, 69, 79, 80, 82, 83, 85, 89, 95, 97, 99, 100, 102-105, 107-109, 111, 113, 116, 123, 125, 127, 130, 131, 152, 154-159, 164, 166, 167-169, 171, 183, 185, 186
Han River 83, 84, 89, 132, 133, 152
Hanson, Anne (Mrs. Østen) 31, 34
Hanson. Martin Gustav 62, 135, 144, 159
Hanson, Østen 29-34, 54, 56, 59, 86, 93, 94, 135
Harrisville, Lars 61
Hatlestad, Iver Christian Larson 44, 61
Hattrem, Miss and Mrs. 80
Hauge, Hans Nielsen 46, 130
Hauge Congregation 130
Haugean 22, 33, 51, 62, 73
Haugerud, Mathilde 92, 111
Hauge Seminary 23
Hauge Synod 6, 23, 24, 28, 29, 35, 36, 40, 42, 51-53, 55, 57, 58, 60-63, 79, 84, 89, 93, 112, 117, 122, 128, 134, 135, 137, 138, 144, 146, 150, 151, 154, 155, 159, 160, 165, 172, 176, 184, 191, 193-198, 200n40, 204n190
Haystack Oath 55
Health of Missionaries 94, 97, 101, 104, 114, 126-27, 178, 187
Hedenström, Miss 50
Helgeson 80, 152
Himle, Edwin 163, 164, 183, 186, 187, 197
Himle, Gidske 104, 118, 139, 155-157, 161, 162, 164, 177, 190, 194
Himle, Thorstein 34, 136, 139, 154, 159, 165, 178, 182, 185, 189, 194, 196
Hjermstad, Mathilda 60-62, 66
Hodnefield, Olava 92, 107-109, 117, 120, 122, 129, 134, 142, 145, 148, 151-153, 166, 169-171, 175-178, 185, 186,188, 190-192, 195
Hoel Parish 49

Hogstad, Johan Peter 42
Holmberg, Alice 193
Holter, Christian Christopherson 61, 63
Homestead Act 30
Hong Kong 14, 71
Hong Xiuquan 14
Hørte Rønning, Gunhild 194
Hotvedt, J. M. J. 139
Huashan 152
Hubei Province 89, 113, 119
Hunan Province 114
Hupeh province 204n190

I

Idols 14, 67, 70, 117, 175, 182, 185, 187
Infanticide 24, 104, 108
Inter-synodical Mission 44
International Woman's Congress 173
Inwood, Iowa 41, 135, 138

J

Jackson, Minnesota 53
Jakobson, Anna Sofie 21
Japan 69, 73-76, 108, 121, 138, 139, 151, 152
Johansen, Anders Daniel 113
John, Griffith 89, 90, 95, 97, 99, 101, 102, 130
Johnsen, Gertine 145, 186
Johnson, Sister Caroline 142, 143
Johnson, Ludvig 79, 81, 97, 114, 202n103
Judson, Adoniram 41
Julotta 87
Junior Mission Band 62

K

Kenyon 28, 32, 128
Kielland, Gustava 20, 37-41, 144
Kim Ok-gyun 139
Kinamissionæren 9, 26, 28, 55, 57, 58, 60, 62-64, 70, 91-93, 100, 104, 108, 111, 129-131, 134, 137, 143, 174, 179, 190, 191
Kivle Werdal, Mabel 3
Kivle Werdal, Marion 3
Kivle Northvedt, Mathilda 3
Kivle Larson, Myrtle 3
Kivle, Per and Torveig 3
Kivle, Svein 3, 8
Kobe Maru 74, 75
Kobe College for Women 75
Kongsberg, Norway 19
Korea 139, 151
Kristenson, Lars Mrs. 167, 168
Kristiansand, Norway 21, 53
Kuling 101

KwaZulu 20

L

Ladies Aid 7, 12, 34, 36-43, 48, 57, 58, 62, 130, 169, 172, 181, 184, 200n37
Landahl, Carl W. 139, 154-164, 166-173, 177, 178, 181-190, 193
Landstad, Magnus Brostrup 20
Lange, A. H. 112
Laohoutian 151
Larvig, Norway 19
Liang Fa 14
Liangyang 177
Li Hongzhang 66, 144, 173
Liu-ho-keo 183
Living God 59, 67, 71, 81, 87, 120, 124, 156,
London Bible Society 14
London Missionary Society 89, 176
Lutheraneren 45, 51-53, 55, 160
Lyngdal 20

M

Ma 117
Madagascar 20, 33, 42, 45, 135
Madland, Caroline 41
Mahtomedi, Minnesota 52
Manchu 14, 148
Mandarin 13-15, 91, 113, 116, 119, 133, 145, 151, 173, 185
Marco Polo 17
McCreary amendment 110
Meningitis 189
Meyer, Lucy Rider 47
Middle Kingdom 15, 121, 139
Mino-Owari Earthquake 74
Missionary Review of the World 45, 47, 96
Missionary Salary 18, 117
Mission Centennial 1888 35, 44
Mission Dove Society 64, 137, 191, 194
Missionsdueforening 64
Mission Society in America 9, 55
Mongolia 17, 19, 90, 146, 196, 197
Moody, Dwight L. 19, 35
Munch, Edvard 49
Murdoch, Dr. 46

N

Nagasaki 76, 152
Nanjing 15, 50, 61
  Treaty of 14, 18
NanLofo temple 185
Nazareth Congregation 61-64, 86, 107
Nelson, Daniel 52, 55, 58, 82, 83, 95, 97, 99, 100, 102, 104, 108, 109, 113, 123, 129, 133, 156, 167, 168, 195

Index | 211

Nelson, Norah 104, 120, 122, 123, 138, 167
Nerve Fever 156
Nestegaard, Ole Syversen, Sr. 49-52, 54, 56, 59, 60, 62, 68, 70, 72, 90, 96, 99, 100, 146, 150, 151, 196, 197, 205n205
Nestegaard, Ole Syversen, Jr. 49, 53, 54, 57, 58, 82, 90, 99, 100, 146, 196
Nestorian Christians 17
Netland, Oline Hermanson 92, 107-109, 111, 115, 118, 120, 122, 124, 126, 129, 132, 134, 135, 140, 142, 146, 166, 203, 204, 208
Netland, Sigfrid 122, 126, 156
Netland, Sigvald 53, 54, 57, 58, 78, 83, 85, 87-89, 92, 97, 98, 102, 108, 109, 113, 119, 121-123, 125, 126, 129, 132, 133, 135, 136, 140, 144-146, 152, 164, 166
New Year celebrations 88, 163
New York Tribune 66
Ningbo 18
Norrise-Armstrong, Maria 46
North China Daily 76
Northfield, Massachusetts 35
Norwegian Danish Augustana Synod 44, 112
Norwegian Evangelical Lutheran Church 53, 55
Norwegian Mission Society 21, 37, 44, 45, 59, 204n190
Norwegian Synod 21, 22, 38, 44, 55, 71, 160
Nüchuang 159
Nyholm. 114, 115

O

Ocean Grove, New Jersey 35
Oceanic 71
Odansan 184
Oftedal, Sven 8, 22, 23
Olmsted County 24, 31, 34
Omaha, Nebraska 35, 68, 69
Opium 14, 17, 53, 91, 179, 186
Oppegaard, A. Ole 55, 57, 62, 112, 135, 145, 169
Order of Salvation 26, 27
Ordo salutis 27
Oscar I 38
Ossian, Iowa 61
Østby, Ole A. 52, 54, 55, 57, 62, 67, 68, 86, 88, 91, 93, 95, 97, 99, 103, 113, 135, 146, 150, 151, 196
Ottesen, Realf 38
Our Savior's Lutheran Church, Inwood, Iowa 41, 135

P

Panic of 1893 116, 144
Pescadores 151
Pietist 26, 27, 31, 130
Pope Innocent 17
Preus, Herman Amberg 44, 144, 199

Q

Qing Dynasty 13, 14, 139, 148
Qufu 123, 138

R

Radcliffe, Reginald 20-22, 35
Radcliff, Iowa 52, 55, 62
Rasmussen, Theodor and Elisabeth 21
Red Wing Seminary 23, 24, 26-28, 34, 54, 139, 157, 158
Reuter Smith, Sofie Dorothea 20, 21, 27, 41-43
Ricci, Matteo 17
Riverside congregation, Dawson, Minnesota 62
Rock River, Wisconsin 38
Røkke, Lavine 92
Roland, Iowa 43
Rønning, Chester 10, 194
Rønning, Halvor 6, 9-11, 19, 22-24, 26, 28, 29, 31, 32, 34, 40, 50, 55-57, 59-62, 64, 67-69, 71-77, 79, 80, 81, 83, 85-87, 89-95, 97-102, 104,107, 109, 113, 114, 116, 119-123, 125, 126, 128, 129, 131-134, 136, 137, 139, 140, 145, 146, 151, 152, 154, 155, 157-159, 162, 164, 166, 169, 173, 177, 182-184, 193, 194
Rønning, Hannah Rorem 62-64, 66-68, 70-73, 75, 83, 85-88, 92, 94-98, 107, 108, 117, 120-123, 126, 134, 137, 139, 143, 151, 154, 158, 161, 163, 165, 166, 169, 176, 178-181, 183-185, 188, 189, 193, 194, 207n275
Rønning, Marie 23, 34
Rønning, Nilius 108, 126, 134, 152, 154, 156, 169, 171, 183, 184, 185
Rønning, Nils 8, 11, 27-31, 34, 68, 95, 150, 155, 156
Rorem, Tom 194
Rushford, Minnesota 58

S

Saint Olaf College 48, 137, 194
Saint Paul, Minnesota 35, 60
Salaries 18, 117
Samtalemøde 64
Sandven, Jørgen Nelson 40
San Francisco 35, 54, 68-71, 74, 107, 108, 112

Santal Mission 49
Schauffler, Mrs. Adolf 115
Schreuder, Hans Paluden Smith 20, 21, 24
Selskap 37
Shaanxi 89
Shangchuan 17
Shanghai 18, 42, 53, 71, 74, 75, 78, 79, 83, 89, 94, 99, 108, 115, 121, 139, 143, 152, 155-157, 159, 161-164, 174, 193, 198
Shangkow 168, 169
Shanxi 100, 119
Shouyun 133
Shogun 76
Siam 105
Sino-Japanese War 138, 204n168
Sje-liang 182, 183
Sjøquist, Missionary 159
Skien, Norway 19, 22, 23
Skordal, Johan 173, 202n103
Skrefsrud, Lars 49
Small Catechism 183
Smith, Stanley 42, 200n39
Society of Jesus 17, 199n1
Solør congregation 24, 31, 40, 57, 61, 62
Songdal 53
South Friborg 150
St. John's College 159
St. Paul's Church in Minneapolis 60
Stavanger Mission High School 22, 23, 43, 50
Storjohann, Johan 49
Stub, Hans Andreas 21
Studd, Charles T. 52
Summer Palace 15, 139
Sungpu, Hubei province 113
Sungpu Affair 114, 123, 125,
Sun Yatsen 121, 148
Sutro Heights Park 70
Svenska Missionen i Kina 100
Sverdrup, Georg 22, 23, 45
Swalestuen, Jørgen Danielson 151
Swallow, Dr. Robert 74, 76
Swedish Mission in China 100

T
Ta-fo-ti 89, 99
Ta-Tung 80
Taipingdian 162, 168, 169, 172, 175, 177, 181-183, 185, 187, 189, 191
Taiping Rebellion 14, 66
Tang, Mr. 99, 117
Tang Dynasty 17
Taylor, James Hudson 9, 13, 14, 16, 18-21, 24, 25, 27, 35, 36, 41, 42, 44, 48, 50, 52, 53, 56, 64, 74, 78, 79, 85, 91, 96, 102, 104, 127, 146, 160, 196, 199n14
Telemark, Norway 6, 8, 11, 23, 30, 70
Thompson, Dr. 167
Ting 113, 114, 124, 125
Tinn, Norway 23, 24
Townsend, General Ward Frederick 16
Treaty of Nanjing see Nanjing
Treaty of Shimonoseki 151
Trinity Congregation, Minneapolis 130
Typhus 94, 156

U
Umatendhjwaze 20
United Church 22, 54, 55, 112, 134, 135, 160
United Norwegian Lutheran Church in America 55

V
Vay, Count Peter de Vaya 84

W
Waitlow, John 159
Wanamingo, Minnesota 24, 29
Wang, Sun 95, 133
Weenaas, August 23, 24, 199n5
Werdal, Joseph 3
Werdal, Morris 3, 9
Wikholm Otto Frederick 113
Williams College 55
Willing Workers 125
Women's Congress of Mission 115
Women's suffrage 130
Wuchang 57, 58, 82-85, 93, 97, 99, 102, 114
Wuxue 66, 80, 99

X
Xavier, St. Francis 17

Y
Yamen, Chong Li 197
Yang 178-181
Yangzi River 14, 50, 66, 78, 80, 83-85, 89
Yellow Sea 76
Yellowstone Journal 91
Yokohama, Japan 71, 74

Z
Zhang Zhidong 114, 119
Zionsforeningen 129
Zion Society for Israel 129

www.ingramcontent.com/pod-product-compliance
Lightning Source LLC
Chambersburg PA
CBHW050316120526
44592CB00014B/1933